MONASTIC WISDOM SERIES: NUMBER TWO

Jean-Marie Howe, OCSO

Secret of the Heart
Spiritual Being

MONASTIC WISDOM SERIES

Patrick Hart, ocso, General Editor

Advisory Board

Michael Casey, ocso   Terrence Kardong, osb
Lawrence S. Cunningham   Kathleen Norris
Bonnie Thurston   Miriam Pollard, ocso

MONASTIC WISDOM SERIES: NUMBER TWO

Secret of the Heart
Spiritual Being

by
Jean-Marie Howe, OCSO

Preface by
André Louf, OCSO

Translated by
Kathleen Waters, OCSO

CISTERCIAN PUBLICATIONS
Kalamazoo, Michigan

Originally published as *Le secret du cœur: l'être spirituel*
© 1999 Abbaye cistercienne Notre-Dame-du-Lac
© Translation copyright, Cistercian Publications 2005

Cistercian Publications

Editorial Offices
The Institute of Cistercian Studies
Western Michigan University
Kalamazoo, Michigan 49008-5415
cistpub@wmich.edu

The work of Cistercian Publications is made possible in part by support from Western Michigan University to The Institute of Cistercian Studies.

CISTERCIAN PUBLICATIONS BOOKS ARE AVAILABLE
AT THE FOLLOWING ADDRESSES:

The United States and Canada: Liturgical Press
Saint John's Abbey   Collegeville, MN 56321-7500
sales@litpress.org

The United Kingdom and Europe: The Columba Press
55A Spruce Avenue
Stillorgan Industrial Park
Blackrock, Co. Dublin Ireland
info@columba.ie

The editors of Cistercian Publications
express their heartfelt appreciation to
Dr. Susan Hubert
for her help in preparing this manuscript for publication.

Library of Congress Cataloging-in-Publication Data

Howe, Jean-Marie.
  [Secret du cœur. English]
  Secret of the heart : spiritual being / Jean-Marie Howe ; preface by André Louf ; translated by Kathleen Waters.
    p. cm. — (Monastic wisdom series ; no. 2)
  Summary: "Considers that through immersion in monastic life, at the level of the heart, persons enter into contact with the mystery of Christ and give birth to spiritual being; discusses prayer and lectio divina"—Provided by publisher.
  Includes bibliographical references and index.
  ISBN-13: 978-0-87907-002-1 (pbk. : alk. paper)
  ISBN-10: 0-87907-002-1 (pbk. : alk. paper)
  1. Monastic and religious life.   2. Spiritual life—Catholic Church.
I. Title.   II. Series.

BX2435.H6313 2005
248.8'943—dc22

                                                        2005010615

Printed in the United States of America

"We dance round in a ring and suppose

but the Secret

sits in the middle and knows."

Robert Frost

TABLE OF CONTENTS

TRANSLATOR'S NOTE

The following conferences were translated from the original French text published by Abbaye Notre-Dame-du-Lac in "Collection Voix monastiques."

Having had the opportunity to consult with the author throughout this undertaking and with her consent, I have made some minor alterations in the English text. For the sake of emphasis and continuity throughout the text, I have employed *italic* type to highlight key words and concepts. All such changes have been made in the service of clarity and pedagogy.

All translations of French citations are the translator's unofficial renderings.

Kathleen Waters, OCSO

AUTHOR'S NOTE

The following conferences were given as a retreat at the monastery of Sainte Marie du Mont (Mont-des-Cats) in France during March of 1997. The conversational style of the original text has been maintained.

Although the material covered in these talks is oriented toward monastic life and often toward Cistercian monastic life in particular, my central point is the existence of *another order* in Christian spiritual life and the *spiritual being* which flows from it. The overall horizon transcends monastic life and is therefore applicable to Christian life in general. It seems important to emphasize this fact from the outset to insure that, in the reader's mind, the scope of this spiritual vision not be limited to monastic life.

I remain deeply indebted to all those persons without whom these conferences would never have existed.

J-MH

PREFACE

There is quite a paradox inherent in our society, and in the type of human beings it produces—persons who are at one and the same time outwardly oriented toward so many points of interest unfolding before their eyes, while secretly attracted inward, tormented as they are by a thirst whose meaning escapes them. They are half-disappointed by the outer world that leaves them dissatisfied, and half-attracted by an inner world whose path of entry has disappeared in the sand. The pain of such inner division causes some to fear anything that reminds them of their interiority, numbing themselves with a thousand distractions that promise to spare them from having to attend to the essential.

The acknowledgement of this state of affairs is doubly painful for believers and followers of Jesus. Had he not himself proclaimed that his Kingdom is not of this world (Lk 17:21) but rather is within (Jn 8:36)? Like so many of their contemporaries, they, too, willingly linger in the outer world and finish by forgetting about the treasure they carry hidden within their hearts. This treasure, Mother Jean-Marie calls her "secret," a term also employed in the Gospel. Even more painful is this realization for today's "contemplative" monks and nuns who, in principle, had left behind so many things that at one time seemed futile and uninteresting to them but who, in their turn and despite themselves, now feel caught up in a world that pursues them even within their monastic enclosure. And yet, has not the whole of monastic tradition, following Origen and Augustine, clearly marked out for them this "path toward the interior," luring them as to a wellspring of great sweetness: "Quanto interius tanto dulcius,": "The further you go within yourselves, the sweeter becomes the path."

We could, of course, advance many theories to account for this painful rending, this strange interior tension, characterized by so many ambiguities which finish by paralyzing the best of intentions. The outer world, now within anybody's reach, has rarely ever been so captivating. The rather abstruse vocabulary of the spiritual tradition of the Fathers of Antiquity, so out of step with present-day terminology, is hardly conducive to in-depth study of their message. And to these we could no doubt add a further reason, one that is perhaps the most decisive: lack of concrete experience. Were we not taken up—and legitimately so—with too many other problems to be venturing forth onto this "interior path"?

Mother Jean-Marie's testimony brings a promising corrective to these insufficiencies. Her book presents the retreat conferences she gave at Mont-des-Cats, in the north of France, where I had the joy of inviting her.

Of course, as she herself reminds us, these conferences do not constitute a course in monastic spirituality, which would have to deal with the writings of authors from the period of the Desert Fathers or from the Cistercian twelfth century. Such works do not appear in this book. On the contrary, other citations appear frequently, taken from contemporary philosophers and novelists. The surprising thing is that the intuitions of these writers, subtly brought out by the author, coincide with the most traditional themes. There is, for example, the theme of pilgrimage toward the inner place of the heart, a unique voyage, adapted to each person's vocation. On this journey, monastics —but also all believers—move forward patiently, while imperceptibly a marvelous transformation is taking place, one that brings them closer to the Lord and to their brothers and sisters, conferring upon them a spiritual priesthood of communion and intercession to the benefit of the whole world.

Mother Jean-Marie thus provides us with a new vocabulary, one which privileges symbols over concepts, a vocabulary at times daringly inventive, which, we hope, will allow modern readers to embark upon a spiritual adventure without the risk of being turned off by an obsolete terminology or mindset. Finally, let us not fail to mention the strength of conviction she conveys, revealing a personal experience that is likely to be infectious.

André Louf, OCSO

INTRODUCTION

One of the best known of the Desert Fathers of fourth-century Egypt, Saint Sarapion the Sidonite, travelled once on pilgrimage to Rome. Here he was told of a celebrated recluse, a woman who lived always in one small room, never going out. Sceptical about her way of life—for he was himself a great wanderer—Sarapion called on her and asked: "Why are you sitting here?" To this she replied: "I am not sitting, I am on a journey."

> I am not sitting, I am on a journey. Every Christian may apply these words to himself or herself. To be a Christian is to be a traveler. Our situation, says the Greek Fathers, is like that of the Israelite people in the desert of Sinai: we live in tents, not houses, for spiritually we are always on the move. We are on a journey through the inward spaces of the heart, a journey not measured by the hours of our watch or the days of the calendar, for it is a journey out of time into eternity.[1]

These words of Kallistos Ware suggest the central idea of this book, with the nuance being that, for me, the Christian journey is a journey not only toward Eternity but at the same time toward *spiritual being*. My hope is that we can make this journey together through the interior spaces of our heart.

We will begin with a discussion of "The Secret." This image, borrowed from a sculpture by Rodin of the same name, I use for the purpose of sharing with you some of my thoughts on the

---

1. Kallistos Ware, *The Orthodox Way*. (Crestwood, NY: St. Vladimir's Seminary Press, 1986) 7.

subject of *being*, particularly *spiritual being*. Two conferences on prayer follow, in the chapter entitled "Heart of Prayer." The impetus for approaching this topic was the questioning brought about by the tragedy which occurred in 1996 at our monastery in Algeria, Notre-Dame-de-l'Atlas.[2] In the next talk, *"Missa sine Nomine,"* we will consider the matter of "spiritual priesthood," which, in the realm of grace, is the fruit of a fullness of *spiritual being:* an outpouring of being, a mediation made possible by the inbreaking of a spiritual order. The next two subjects will lead us more specifically into our monastic lifestyle: the cenobitic and contemplative dimensions of Cistercian life. First, in a conference entitled "Mundane Culture–Heart Culture," we will consider some of the tensions between the worlds in which we live. This will be followed by a look at our "Contemplative Identity and *Lectio Divina*." I would also like to share with you a reflection on the subject of the *elemental* which I have entitled "In Contact with the Elemental–Absorbed by the Divine." This reflection on the *elemental* is a prelude to our viewing the film *Babette's Feast,* and the following chapter, "If Only You Knew What God Is Offering," focuses specifically on the message of that film as it relates to the main themes of this book. In the final conference, "Soulscape," we will consider the uniqueness of each person's journey through the *heart* into *"another order."*

Basically, the vision I hope to transmit is quite simple: through *immersion* in monastic life we enter into *contact* with the Mystery of Christ, a contact which takes place at the level of the *heart* and gives birth to *spiritual being*. This *processus,* this progression, implies a transformation of being: its awakening, growth, and effusion. Here we find the deepest dynamic of monastic spiritual life: a contact with *"another order"* that transforms the person at the level of *being* like "iron in the fire!"

---

2. Seven Cistercian monks of the monastery of Notre-Dame de l'Atlas in Algeria were taken hostage by Islamic terrorists in March 1996, and murdered by them on May 21st of that year.

1

THE SECRET

In Auguste Rodin's sculpture "The Secret," a symbol of the secret—whatever it may be for the artist—is preciously enclosed between two clasped hands which are sculpted in an upright position. A photograph of this sculpture has served as a symbol of what I have come to perceive as my own "secret." This secret is not something esoteric and accessible only to the "initiated," yet it does seem somewhat elusive when I open my clasped hands and try to share it with others. It is as though it slips through my fingers, leaving me standing there, apparently empty-handed. I have come here to Mont-des-Cats bearing this secret, hopeful that I will be able to share it with you but also mindful of the risk I run of appearing to be empty-handed.

I am neither an orator nor a scholar. I do not possess a wealth of knowledge that I can unveil before you. I have only an intuition, which over the years has grown into a conviction, perhaps even a "holy obsession!" In keeping with the earliest monastic tradition, I have only "a word" to offer, and that only if someone should happen to ask. By inviting me to give this retreat, Dom André Louf, your abbot, has asked, and because he has been supportive of my efforts to communicate this "word" in the preface he wrote to my first book (a preface which is better than the book itself!), I dare attempt once again to articulate my secret.

If you are at all familiar with my previous book, *Spiritual Journey: The Monastic Way*, please forgive the inevitable repetitions that will appear throughout these conferences. As I have only one message, which was basically articulated in that book, what I say here will have a familiar ring to it and perhaps seem

1

no more than a "variation on a theme." While it may not provide new material for your mind, it may resonate nonetheless in your deep *heart*.

Let me begin by sharing with you my *secret*. There exists in the spiritual life what I have come to refer to as *another order*. There it is! My secret! Simple. I could stop now. I have uttered my word, my message, my intuition, my "holy obsession." This is the reality that I sought to transmit in *Spiritual Journey*, but one never knows how successful such attempts are. The book was well received, and I hope some heard the echo of a consciousness that there is *another order* in the Christian spiritual life (and hence in our Cistercian monastic life) to which we can and should aspire.

As I explained in the Author's Note to *Spiritual Journey*, the constant that underlies the doctrine treated in that book is the growth of *spiritual being*, and this applies to all forms of Christian life.[1] My primary intention was to bring to light the reality of *spiritual being* as well as the importance of its awakening and growth in the spiritual life. The message of that book—and this—is presented from a monastic perspective simply because it is the one most familiar to me and it is therefore natural that I would map out the journey to the goal through the monastic lifestyle. And what exactly is that goal? In essence, it is the awakening and growth of our innate capacity for God, mediated through an immersion in the Mystery of Christ, facilitated by an assimilation of the Word of God, and leading to a transformation of being. The journey described may at first glance seem to apply exclusively to a monastic context but is, in actuality, universal. This is not to imply that monastic life is not important to the journey toward spiritual being; it is, on the contrary, very important. I believe that monastic spirituality is an elemental spirituality, which means that it is reduced to the essential. I also believe that there is a connaturality between the elemental and the divine. This elemental spiritual life, which is ours, is a simple reality: a state of being, engaged in a continual

---

1. Jean-Marie Howe, *Spiritual Journey: The Monastic Way* (Petersham, MA: St. Bede's Publications, 1989) xi.

yet imperceptible process of transformation—a spiritual transformation at the level of *being*. It was and is by virtue of Cistercian monastic life thus conceived that the consciousness that there is *another order* came to light in me.

Spiritual Journey treats monastic life mainly from the perspective of my own journey, but the real message of the book is that, in living the elemental spirituality that is Cistercian monastic life—a spirituality where everything is oriented toward the emergence of the essential—a *consciousness* was awakened in me. It could be said that the essential emerged in my personal discovery of the existence of *another order* in the spiritual life and the *transformation of being* inherent in our contact with it. Understood in this way, monastic life is seen to foster an awareness and an experience of spiritual realities, spiritual realities that are equally present at the heart of all Christian life. In other words, a consciousness or an experience of something *"other"* can emerge from within the monastic context, but it should not be confused with or confined to that context. The monastic way of life is at the service of, and in some way contains, this deeper reality; it is, however, *this reality*, and not monastic life *per se*, that I hoped to highlight in my previous book.

In drawing your attention to *Spiritual Journey*, I am not attempting to indulge myself in some illusory vainglory at having been "published." Quite the contrary. I refer to that book simply because its subject matter is the foundation of what I will be saying here. I may not discuss the topics of the book with the same depth and precision, but I will elaborate on several of their key aspects. I hope to elicit, however faintly, a glimmer of a consciousness that is *"other,"* a consciousness of a level of *being* that is *"other,"* and a consciousness of what I could perhaps call an ontological spiritual reality.

I would like to continue this conference by speaking a bit about the concept of *being*. As you have no doubt already ascertained, this concept is central not only to my vision of monastic life but also to my vision of spiritual life. Rest assured, however, that my discourse will be far from metaphysical! What interests me is the relationship between *being* and the spiritual life. In my estimation, the "real" exists only at the level or in the realm of *being,* and it is the real that draws me in the spiritual life. Let us first consider the mystery of *being* in general.

The phrase "to have being" seems to me to imply that the *being* of a person is in contact with the *being* of someone or something else. This contact, a dynamic that takes place at the level of the *heart,* gives one substance, density, roots—*being.* To find a quality of *being* in a person, even outside of a specifically spiritual context, is already something special. In his novel *Citadelle,* Antoine de Saint-Exupéry speaks of a man who carries a tree in his heart.[2] In the process of fascinatedly watching a tree grow inside an abandoned house, the being of this man was, so to speak, bound to the *being* of the tree. They were in contact. In this way, the man possessed a substance which other men, who listened to him speak about his tree, did not possess.

In his book *L'Absurde et le Mystère,* Jean Guitton describes the phenomenon in this way:

> In speaking to you, Criton, I do not know if it is my speech that goes before me or if it is my thought that precedes my speech; and both run after each other in an endless circuit. But this cavalcade hides something more intimate; for at the same time that I assemble concepts and order them, there is in me a faculty that is like the eye of my eye, the ear of my ear, the intellect of my intellect. I do not know how to refer to it. Call it, if you wish, by this vague word "heart," the faculty that, through concepts, mysteriously unites the intimate reality that is in me to the intimate reality hidden in things. This profound process is true knowledge. It leads me toward *being:* by that I mean that beyond that which is conceived, I am led to the reality. This reality, we call *being,* and in the Greek language this word *being* is simple: it has one letter in the form of an open mouth, called "omicron," and another letter, in the shape of a cup ready to receive liqueur, which is called "nu." It is therefore "ON," *Being*—that toward which intuition tends. It is for me the heart of things, toward which my own heart

2. Antoine de Saint-Exupéry, *Citadelle* (Paris: Gallimard, 1948) 62–63. Translated by Stuart Gilbert, *The Wisdom of the Sands* (New York: Harcourt, Brace and Co., 1950; Chicago: University of Chicago Press, 1979) 46.

tends, and the union of this heart to that heart, I call knowledge.[3]

Guitton refers to this level of *being* as the "heart" and defines *being* itself as the intimate reality of something or someone. *Being* is the reality found at the core of a concept, an object, or a subject. It is toward the *being* of things that our *being* tends for a union that gives birth to real knowledge or, better yet, knowledge of the real. I consider this to be the truest dynamic of the spiritual life.

Unfortunately, we usually remain more or less on the surface: of things, of people, and of ourselves. We are not in contact with our own *being*, the *being* of things, or the deep reality of what is happening at a given moment. Our relationship with it all is not true, is not real. Consequently, our *being* lacks substance, density. If one transposes this fact to the spiritual world, it is even more striking, more disconcerting.

In the context of this conference, *being* is understood as an affair of the *heart*, but there are also levels in the *heart*. Whenever we allude to the spiritual we are manifestly referring to the profoundest levels of the heart. It seems to me, in fact, that to have spiritual *being*, the deep *heart* must be awakened. The intimate sense (the *sens intime*) of spiritual realities must be awakened. There is in the deep *heart* a profound affinity by which our *being* attaches itself to, connects with, and comes into contact with spiritual realities. It is at this level that one can find an ontological attachment or, so to speak, a connection to God.

In monastic life, we speak of the "return to the *heart*" *(reditus ad cor)*, the "life of the *heart*," and "finding the place of the *heart*." In essence, to find one's *heart* is to find one's *being*, for the heart "senses" or "picks up" *being*. Monastic life is full of *being*, filled as it is with spiritual realities, because it is filled with the Mystery of Christ. The awakened *heart* is attuned to *being*, attuned to the intimate reality contained therein, for the *heart* is a spiritual organ, a sort of radar that senses the spiritual wherever it

3. Jean Guitton, *L'Absurde et le Mystère* (Paris: Desclée de Brouwer, 1984) 22–23.

is. Thus, the deep *heart* roots itself in *being,* whence comes its substance and a real attachment to God. It is by virtue of this contact with God that we are transformed, *real*-ly.

I cannot let this opportunity pass without alluding to the colorful metaphor employed by Simone Weil to explain this type of transformation and also to unmask any illusions in this area. Allow me to quote just a bit of her text:

> There is no fire in a cooked dish, but one knows it has been on the fire.

> On the other hand, even though one may think to have seen the flames under them, if the potatoes are raw it is certain they have not been on the fire.

> It is not by the way a man talks about God, but by the way he talks about things of the world that best shows whether his soul has passed through the fire of the love of God. In this manner no deception is possible. There are false imitations of the love of God, but not of the transformation it effects in the soul, because one has no idea of this transformation except by passing through it oneself. . . .

> But, like a woman's pregnancy, this transformation is not effected by direct efforts, but by a union of love with God.[4]

This loving union is what Saint Exupéry and Guitton call *contact with* and indicates a union at the level of the *heart,* a substantial union that gives *being* and transforms the person. Persons transformed in this manner carry God, the Beloved, within their *hearts.* The words, actions, and even the mere presence of such persons has, as a direct result of coming into contact with *the* Other, a weight or a density that is *"other."*

In the language of our Cistercian spirituality, one could say that our ontological attachment to God, at the level of the *heart,* will transform the image of God that we are into the likeness of God that we were born to be. This is the growth of *spiritual being.*

---

4. Simone Weil, *La Connaissance Surnaturelle* (Paris: Gallimard, 1950) 96. Translated by Richard Rees, *First and Last Notebooks* (London: Oxford University Press, 1970) 145–46.

2

HEART OF PRAYER

Part One

Huambo, Bosnia, Nishinomya, Kikwit, Atlas, Mokoto, La Clarté-Dieu. Monasteries of our Order around the globe are being plunged into the throes of misery: civil war, fratricide, earthquakes, epidemics, terrorism, exiles, famine, violence, hatred, murder. The suffering of the world—the suffering of our Order.

Since the General Chapter of 1993 our solidarity with human suffering seems to have become much more intense because so many communities of our Cistercian family have been or still are on the front lines of the crises that daily assail our world. The once faceless masses of suffering people now have names; they are truly our brothers and sisters. In the measure that the Order grows, the world becomes smaller. We are experiencing in dramatic ways the reality that we are indeed all one family, all one people. We are no longer sympathetic observers of these catastrophes; we are implicated emotionally and spiritually—perhaps more than ever before. The suffering of the world has entered our cloisters in brutal and poignant ways over the course of these past few years. The tragedy of Atlas is certainly one of the most powerful examples of this state of affairs.

In March 1996, horrific news was disseminated throughout our monasteries as well as throughout the world: our brothers had been taken hostage by terrorists! Our brothers. Hostages. Terrorists. Daily we prayed, daily we offered intercessory prayers at the Divine Office: "for the monks of Atlas," "for our brothers of Atlas," "for the release of the monks of Atlas," "for the families of the monks," "for the Church in Algeria," and finally the heart-rending "for our deceased brothers of Notre-Dame de l'Atlas, let us pray to the Lord."[1]

One thing all these events have in common is that they have brought us face to face with many mysteries: the mysteries of suffering, evil, human solidarity, and, perhaps the most personal of all, the mystery of our own vocation. What is our response, what is our responsibility as monks, when confronted with such anguish, such misery, such need? During those weeks of intense prayer for our brethren of Atlas, prayer that united the entire Order in a profound *intentio cordis*, I could not help but grapple with the very mystery of prayer, as it was essentially our sole means of responding.

What is the relationship between prayer and the monastic life? What *is* prayer? What *is* monastic life? What, for that matter, *is* a monk? Questions. *Questions* that catalyze a quest for answers. But these answers lay shrouded in the realm of mystery.

I remember a retreat in which the distinction was made between a problem and a mystery. A problem must be solved. A mystery must be lived. A problem can engender frustration. A mystery can engender fascination.

I am convinced that monastic life and spiritual life in general are best envisaged from the vantage point of mystery rather than problem. The two dynamics are very different. Confronted with a reality that we deem to be a "problem," we risk becoming anxious, impatient, aggressive, proud, and controlling in our response to it. Faced with what we come to recognize as a "mystery," we have more latitude to let go and be patient, humble, trusting, and open to awe. A problem demands analysis, action, and resolution: a dynamic I call "swimming."

1. These conferences were originally given in March 1997, a year after seven Cistercian monks of the monastery of Notre-Dame de l'Atlas in Algeria were murdered by militants.

A mystery invites meditation, contemplation, and readiness for revelation: a dynamic I call "immersion."

Should a monk not spontaneously view life through the lens of mystery? Modern secular mentality is more prone to approach things, situations, people, and even God with a "problematic" bias. As we have just seen, problems have to be solved regardless of their nature (material, psychological, social, institutional, spiritual, or otherwise). And yet the more one learns, through experience, that truth—or let us call it wisdom—is acquired at the price of humility, the more capable one will be of contemplating rather than analyzing the deep mystery underpinning all levels of existence. The monk, for whom humility is a pivotal value, should be naturally disposed to such a "mysteric" approach to life.

Mysteries, by their very nature, are beyond our willful grasp. In a way, they impoverish us, eluding, as they do, our desire to control and possess. The realization that our very vocation issues from the ultimate Mystery—unfolding within it, evolving toward it—should give us pause. Monastic life is an entry into the Mystery of Christ and, little by little, this Mystery reveals itself as immense. On the one hand, we must use all our capacities to enter it. On the other hand, we have to recognize that we can never grasp its immensity. What is actually called for is to let ourselves be grasped by it! We are not in charge here. We have been conquered by something "ever-grandlier great," to quote Rilke's poem "The Spectator,"[2] and our *willfulness* must cede dominion to *willingness.*

By approaching monastic life, consciously or unconsciously, as a "problem" that needs to be dissected, scrutinized, and programmed, one risks reducing a transcendent reality to an all-too-human level of comprehension and, in so doing, rendering oneself frustrated and miserable. To approach the same reality with an attitude respectful of its inherent "mystery" is to accept that one can never penetrate its depths by virtue of one's own

2. Rainer Maria Rilke, *Sämtliche Werke, Erster Band* (Insel: Verlag, 1955) 460. Translated by J. B. Leishman, *Selected Works*, vol. 2 (London: Hogarth Press, 1960) 137. The German phrase is "immer Größerem zu sein."

power or effort. A mystery must be lived, and it is precisely in living it that the veil could lift and permit a moment of illumination, insight, or wisdom.

I am reminded of the beautiful words of Abraham Heschel, philosopher and mystic, in an anthology of his writings entitled *I Asked For Wonder.* He seems to be saying something similar, citing "awe" as a precondition for perceiving mystery. Heschel writes:

> Awe is an intuition for the dignity of all things, a realization that things not only are what they are but they also stand, however remotely, for something supreme.
>
> Awe is a sense for the transcendence, for the reference everywhere to the mystery beyond all things. It enables us to perceive in the world intimations of the divine, . . . to sense the ultimate in the common and the simple; to feel in the rush of the passing the stillness of the eternal. What we cannot comprehend by analysis, we become aware of in awe.[3]

Awe . . . humility . . . patience . . . immersion: these attitudes are essential to the contemplation of the mystery that lies below the surface.

I began this digression while I was reflecting on the mystery of prayer within the context of monastic life. In fact, all the elements of this lifestyle, and not just prayer, reveal their true face in the mirror of mystery. It would perhaps be preferable to speak less in terms of monastic "observances" or even "values" and more in terms of monastic "mysteries": the mystery of *lectio divina,* or the liturgy, or the vows; the mystery of community life, and so on. If, as we believe, monastic life is profoundly rooted in the Mystery of Christ, then all the elements of this way of life are signs pointing beyond themselves, directing us toward the *order of mystery.*

Is it not precisely because monastic life, as lived out in daily life, *is* so deeply grounded in the Mystery of Christ that it

---

3. Abraham Heschel, *I Asked For Wonder,* edited by Samuel H. Dresner (New York: Crossroads, 1983) 3. Ellipsis in original.

can be of some consequence for the world at large? Monastic life, so understood, is an immersion in the very life of Christ at the heart of his Mystical Body, the Church. It is from within that Mystery that monastic life can be of service to humanity, in a way we cannot measure, comprehend, or explain. Our life as monks is a life of human and spiritual solidarity with all humanity. Although the intricacies of this bond remain a mystery hidden in God, there are some very concrete exigencies of the bond. The irreducible exigency is *depth.*

Depth is the key to the mystery of the fecundity of a monk's prayer. It is a question of *spiritual being,* that is, the depth of spiritual being. There exists, in the depths of the human *heart,* "something"—call it a seed of divine life—that must be awakened. Once awakened, this seed grows and becomes *spiritual being.* Deepening of being and transformation of being go together hand in hand. Thus it could be said that everything depends upon the depth of the person. Depth, which is an initial gift bestowed upon our nature by God, once acknowledged and accepted, can be progressively sounded by the monastic lifestyle and have repercussions far beyond that of the individual monk. If this depth exists within us, all the elements of our monastic life can become, as it were, canals of grace for the salvation and transformation of the world.

To open our *heart,* to open a depth within ourselves: this is the aim of monastic life, and from this flows its fertility. The treasure hidden in the field of monastic life is depth: to arrive at such a depth of being that our whole life flows from the level of the *heart,* for it is there where God is, there where God gives to us and "through" us to the world. The level of the *heart is* the level of prayer.

Monastic life tends toward prayer, above all continual prayer. Continual prayer is not a matter of the constant repetition of prayers; it is to have a *heart of prayer*—which comes from living a life that has been deeply transformed.

During a televised interview made during his visit to Quebec a few years ago, Olivier Clément was asked to sketch a spiritual portrait of the anonymous nineteenth-century "Russian Pilgrim." Clément replied:

A spiritual portrait? I would say that he was self-effacing in his quest. He walked and he walked but essentially it was an inward journey to the ultimate depths of himself where God dwells. The exterior expanse of his pilgrimage is a symbol of the interior space and this is what we sense all along. We sense a man who has an immense need of silence and an immense need of prayer. All he asks is that someone teach him how to pray. . . . He's never happier than when he can stop somewhere . . . and be alone in the silence. It is only at the end of his life that we recognize a man who has been so consumed by the love of God that he no longer has need to seek God, so to speak, because God is there. He is, in a way, immersed in God. It is then that he becomes available to others, as it is now his turn to help them.[4]

And when the interviewer asked what message the "Russian Pilgrim" had for today's world, Clément said:

To seek the place of the heart. We live so much on the surface of ourselves. We live in our head and in our entrails, and all the vast spaces of the heart we have forgotten. I believe that we must rediscover them. . . .[5]

This is what we try to do in monastic life: rediscover the heart, purify it, and rectify it so that our prayer flows from the one source capable of saving this world—the fountain of living waters, the Holy Spirit.

Today, perhaps more than ever, one senses an urgent need for depth, a need which sometimes results in a desperate search for a means to attain it. And yet, the true depth that the human *heart* seeks is not of an intellectual or psychological order and cannot be readily acquired by means of "techniques" or by force of will. It is more often than not the fruit of a long spiritual endeavor. This itinerary is mapped out in a particular manner in the monastic life but is fundamentally the same journey

---

4. Olivier Clément, interviewed on *Second Regard*, Société Radio Canada, 1986.

5. Ibid.

toward depth and toward God, for whom every persons thirsts, consciously or unconsciously.

The spiritual journey that unfolds in monastic life is truly an adventure. The key perhaps is to deepen our present experience day after day, going deeper and deeper, from discovery to discovery, on a path toward the *heart*, which, because of the immanence of God, reveals itself to be infinite, endless, and boundless.

A witness by its very existence to the transcendence and absoluteness of God, monastic life is also a witness, through its intercession, to the immanence of God, an immanence that saves and heals the world. Karl Rahner compared the power of this divine immanence to that of a volcano when he stated:

> [Christ's] resurrection is like the first eruption of a volcano which shows that in the interior of the world God's fire is already burning, and this will bring everything to blessed ardour in his light. He has risen to show that that has already begun. Already from the heart of the world into which he descended in death, the new forces of a transfigured earth are at work. Already in the innermost center of all reality, futility, sin and death are vanquished and all that is needed is the short space of time which we call history *post Christum natum*, until everywhere and not only in the body of Jesus what has really already begun will be manifest.[6]

Paul VI once said that the monk is the sign that there is at work in the world a force that so transcends the limits of this world that it will be capable of transfiguring it on the last day. Such an attestation is not to be taken lightly. It is terribly serious. Yet there is nothing automatic about it. The prayer of the monk and the life of the monk must be rooted in this subterranean mystery: without that, one dare not even speak of intercession.

In an article entitled "God is the Intercessor," Walter Wink made the interesting suggestion that we are always preceded in

---

6. Karl Rahner, *Everyday Faith*. Translated by W. J. O'Hara (New York: Herder and Herder, 1968) 80–81.

our intercessory prayer by God. God is already praying within us. When we begin to pray, we are, so to speak, already at the second stage of prayer. We are joining God in a prayer which is unfolding within us and within the world. Our task in prayer is that of giving voice to the Spirit's groaning within us and bringing the Spirit's utterances to language and conscious awareness.[7]

In the same article, we find an echo of the image Rahner used when describing this mysterious interior force that is at work below the surface, transforming all.

> The Holy Spirit is like a substrate of molten magma under the Earth's crust, trying to erupt volcanically in each of us. It does not have to be invoked, but merely allowed; not called to be present, but acknowledged as present already. Our task is not to mobilize God, but rather to bring our consciousness and commitment to God, to give articulation to the inarticulate groanings within our souls, to bring God's longings to speech.[8]

To intercede means to become a channel of God's own ardent desire for the salvation and divinization of all humanity. Herein lies the ultimate mystery of our vocation.

PART TWO

I trust that what has been said so far has confirmed the idea that prayer beckons us to mysterious depths. Now we will see that those depths are not always consoling to experience. Even so, we need not be disoriented or dismayed by the realization that this descent into the recesses of the human *heart* reveals not only the "groaning of the Spirit" but also the groaning of a nature encrusted in sin, both personal and collective. It is inevitable that any real journey into the depths will disclose not

7. Walter Wink, "God is the Intercessor," *Sojourners* 19.9 (Nov. 1990) 24.
8. Ibid.

only the innate solidarity of our spirit with the Holy Spirit but also the insidious solidarity of human sinfulness.

This gnawing sense of our complicity with sin and evil, not just in specific instances but also on a cosmic plane, brings to our awareness the uncomfortable reality of the human condition. But within this darkness there is light, for this realization also places us at the heart of the redemptive mission of Christ. Reality tells us that sin connects us all; reality tells us that each human being is, at least theoretically, capable of any expression of evil, be it the most horrendous. The Mystery tells us that Christ penetrated into the very core of this somber reality, identifying himself not only with sinners but, as Scripture reveals, with sin itself. The "sinless one" became sin in order to save sinners. Is it unreasonable to expect that we, "bona-fide" sinners who, though far from innocent, are nonetheless disciples of Christ and immersed in his Mystery, would be called upon to identify with and, in union with Christ, assume the sin of the world?

Our prayer, our intercession, becomes all the more poignant and urgent as we are moved not only by the yearnings of the Holy Spirit but also by the yearnings of our captive heart, which groans in unison with all of wounded humanity. We will come to recognize in our own struggle the struggle of our brothers and sisters who also yearn to be liberated from the bonds of corruption and futility that enslave us. And yet, this struggle would be sterile and this aspiration vain, if not for the redemptive struggle of Christ to reconcile sinners with God. The mystery of prayer is a mystery of solidarity, both human and divine.

Jean Lafrance, in a book about prayer of the heart, describes the prayer of Silouan, a saintly Orthodox monk of Mount Athos. To illustrate what I have been saying, allow me to share with you a few excerpts from this book, in which Lafrance witnesses to what he learned from Silouan:

> [H]e made me understand that a man could be transformed into a "living prayer," that his prayer could rise like a pillar of fire up to heaven. But he especially showed me how much *God's love impels us to intercede* for our brothers. . . .

The striking trait in a man like Silouan is his faith in the power of prayer for the world.[9]

And what is prayer for Silouan?

When Silouan prays for his brothers, he never sets himself apart from them; he does not even pray in their name, for he knows very well that only one prayer is always answered, that of Jesus, the Just Man *par excellence* who made himself sin in solidarity with sinners in order to intercede with them and for them.[10]

"The love of God impels us to intercede . . ."; Jesus "made himself sin in solidarity with sinners in order to intercede. . . ." Jesus *is* this love of God that impels us toward the misery of others, the love of God that became identified with our own sins, the love of God that can make of a poor human being a "living prayer."

In the second letter to the Corinthians,[11] Saint Paul makes a remark about people who believe that Jesus died for all in order that all might live in him. He says that the love of God "controls" or "compels" them; some translations use the words *forces, constrains,* or *pushes.* These are strong words; Saint Paul is speaking of an intense interior movement rather than of some vague influence.

What is this love of which he speaks? It is the love that "impelled" Christ to die in order for all to be reconciled with God. "[I]n Christ," Saint Paul goes on to say in verse 19, "God was reconciling the world to himself, not counting anyone's trespasses against them, but entrusting to us a message of reconciliation." The gist of all this seems to be that a Christian, one who "believes" and has "conviction," is called not merely as a

---

9. Jean Lafrance, *Prayer of the Heart.* Translated by Florestine Audette (Sherbrooke, Quebec: Éditions Paulines, 1991) 109–110.

10. Ibid., 111. Italics added.

11. 2 Cor 5:14-15: For the love of Christ controls us, because we are convinced that one has died for all; therefore all have died. And he died for all, that those who live might live no longer for themselves but for him, who for their sake died and was raised.

messenger but also as a "bearer" of the love of Christ and of his reconciliation. In verse 20, we read: "We are the ambassadors of Christ; God makes his appeal *through us*. We beseech you, on behalf of Christ, be reconciled with God." The love of Christ that inspires Christians is a love that seeks the salvation of all humanity. Ultimately, Christians are motivated, perhaps even compelled, not by their love *for* Christ, but by the very love *of* Christ burning within their hearts. To be Christian is to *live Christ's life!*

If one pursues this passage of Scripture a bit further, one finds that the Greek word which is translated as "constrains" or "compels" is used elsewhere with the additional connotation of "anguish" (Lk 12:50; 2 Cor 2:4). This love of Christ is an anguished love; perhaps this is what Pascal meant when he said that Christ would be in agony until the end of the world. The love that compels Christ can know no respite until *all* creation is reconciled with God. To the degree that one can say, "I live now not with my own life but with the life of Christ who lives in me" (Gal 2:20), one will be compelled by this consuming love which gives itself for the salvation of the world. This *anguished love* is the heart of Christian prayer; how much more central should it be to the monk's prayer? In speaking this way, we realize that Christian intercession is intimately associated with the primordial intercession of Christ, identified both with the sin of the world and the loving will of the Father, even to the point of holocaust. Elsewhere in *Prayer of the Heart*, Lafrance writes:

> Without breaking away from the Father with whom he is in constant communion, he made a step which took him to the heart of man and of all the tragic situations, a step from which we will never be able to disengage himself. His step is such that one can no longer speak about God without speaking of man and no longer speak about man without speaking of God. Their destinies are inextricably bound in the Incarnation. *Christ, true man and true God, is totally answerable for man in his sin when he turns to the Father and is totally answerable for God when he turns to man.*[12]

12. Lafrance 117. Italics added.

The prayer of Jesus, the prayer of Silouan, and the prayer of the monk is a prayer of solidarity, not superiority; of identification, not condescendence. As Silouan himself said, "I desire nothing more than to pray for others as I do for myself. To pray for others means *to give the blood of one's own heart.*"[13]

I am reminded here of the words of Dom Christian of Atlas in his "Last Testament." Indeed, Dom Christian was also acutely aware of the mystery of human solidarity. He too knew that, faced with the misery that ravages our world, we cannot content ourselves with some vague solidarity based on abstract altruism but that we must be honest enough and humble enough to admit our complicity in the very evil that underlies so much of that suffering. His words cut to the heart of this mystery:

> My life has no more value than any other.
> Nor any less value.
> In any case it has not the innocence of childhood.
> I have lived long enough to know that I share in the evil
> which seems, alas, to prevail in the world,
> even in that which would strike me blindly.
> I should like, when the time comes, to have a lucidity
> which would allow me to beg forgiveness of God
> and of all my fellow human beings
>   and at the same time to forgive with all my heart
>   the one who would strike me down.[14]

Not many people would readily admit or accept their share of responsibility for the evil that daily affronts us. Not many are willing to look deeply into this mystery of human solidarity, perhaps because in doing so they would risk seeing their own reflection in the dark waters of human misery, not as spectators or victims, but as perpetrators and accomplices. Not many would, but the monk must!

Léon Bloy grasped this mystery of solidarity both in its horror and in its grandeur when he wrote:

---

13. Ibid. 110. Italics added.
14. "Testament of Dom Christian de Chergé," Hallel 21.2 (1996) 150.

Our liberty is interdependent with the equilibrium of the world and this is what we must understand in order not to be astonished by the profound mystery of Reversibility, the philosophical name of the great dogma of the Communion of Saints. Each person who commits a free act projects his personality into infinity. If, with a bad heart, he gives a penny to a pauper, this penny pierces the hand of the poor person, falls, pierces the earth, perforates suns, traverses the heavens and compromises the universe. If a person commits an impure act, it obscures perhaps thousands of hearts that he does not even know but who correspond in some mysterious fashion to him and who need this person to be pure, like a traveler dying of thirst needs the proverbial Gospel glass of water. A charitable act, a movement of true pity sings for him the divine praises, from Adam until the end of time; it heals the sick, consoles the hopeless, appeases tempest, redeems captives, converts the unbelieving and protects the human race.[15]

Returning to Silouan, I again quote Lafrance:

Silouan's prayer for men draws its source from his profound communion with sinners. One day, when he was crushed by trials and temptations of all sorts, he asked the Lord what he must do so that his heart may become humble. And the Lord answered: "Remain in hell in thought and do not lose heart." Like Jesus, he descended into hell and by experiencing his own sin, he shared the anxiety, the suffering and the solitude of his brothers who were far way from God. Then he could cry out to the Father and implore him to have pity and rescue him from the abyss of sin along with all those with whom he was in solidarity.[16]

The monk's identification with the sin of the world is no pious charade; it is a brutal truth. Dom Christian, like Silouan, understood this; he, too, plunged into a hell of hatred, yet did not despair. He, too, was willing to pray with the blood of his

---

15. Léon Bloy, *Le Désespéré* (Paris: Mercure, 1953) 82.
16. Lafrance 112.

own heart for the salvation of his brothers, even though they were the "brothers of the mountain," his term for the Islamic rebels.

> And you also, the friend of my final moment,
> who would not be aware of what you were doing.
> Yes, for you too, I say this THANK YOU and this
> "A-DIEU"—
>
> And may we find each other, happy "good thieves,"
> in Paradise, if it pleases God, the Father of us both.
> AMEN.[17]

To express these ideas on prayer, I have had recourse to the thoughts of many different people, all of whom have brought the light and truth of their experience to bear upon this subject. And yet, are we any closer to understanding the vast mystery that is prayer?

When faced with situations like Atlas, when confronted with the "hushed murmur of immense misery," the only viable response for us as monks, our only authentic means of responding, is prayer. My thought, when living out the tragedy of Atlas, was that the only prayer that I truly desired to offer was the prayer of a life interiorly transformed. If only I could just *be*, here in the monastery, "a living prayer."

There is a stone on my desk; it comes from the Annapolis Valley of Nova Scotia, Canada. For approximately four hundred million years, it was immersed in the depths of existence. Lost in the Annapolis Valley, one could say—geologically—that it lived long silences and profound disturbances. The result? Through a small hole in the stone, one can see sparkling crystals buried deep inside an otherwise ordinary-looking rock, crude and uninteresting. These tiny specks of crystal, perceived only by dint of careful attention, have a captivating beauty about them and have become, for me, a symbol of inner transformation.

---

17. "Testament of Dom Christian" 151.

The true response to our often anguished desire to intervene in the suffering which devastates our world is, in fact, this interior transformation, this birth of *spiritual being* that takes place silently and secretly, in the very heart of our obscurity. This transformation is no mere ideal to which one can aspire but a mystery that can become a reality. This is why the path of *spiritual being* attracts me: its awakening, its growth, and its outpouring into the world.

Another symbol that encompasses this same reality to me is the thurible. A censer set down on the ground remains immobile while it pours fragrant fumes out into the surrounding atmosphere. In *Spiritual Journey*, I explained this symbol in the following way:

> We could just as well speak of the incense of spiritual being simply pouring out of the monk's emptiness into the world—at once adoration and intercession. . . .
>
> This image of the incense of spiritual being pouring out of the monk's emptiness symbolizes what I call a "spiritual priesthood." Capacity, kenosis, rebirth, spiritual being— all lead not only to a personal transformation in Christ, but also to a universal or cosmic transformation of the entire Body of Christ. Our spiritual journey is not simply a personal one. As part of the Mystical Body of Christ, our journey is one with all humanity—past, present, and future. Yet, if in the order of grace we can become channels of grace for others, let us never forget that we also receive.[18]

Georges Bernanos asks, "Who among us is certain of belonging to the Communion of Saints?"

> And if one has this joy, what role does one play therein? Who are the rich and who are the poor in this astonishing community? Who are those who give and who are those who receive? What surprises! . . . Oh! nothing appears more regulated, more strictly ordered, hierarchical, balanced than the exterior life of the Church. But its interior

18. Howe, *Spiritual Journey*, 90–91.

life overflows with the prodigious liberties, one would
almost say extravagances, of the Spirit—the Spirit who
blows where it wishes.[19]

We will never know, at least not in this life, whether grace
did indeed blow *through* us, but we can have the certainty that it
blows *within* us to heal and transform us. We will never know,
here below, if we are among the "givers," but we can have the
certitude that we "receive." Called to holiness, as is each human
being, the monk begins this journey as a sinner, a pardoned
sinner. We must never lose sight of this fact: if we feel the desire
to pray, if we are capable of prayer, if we are capable of anything in the spiritual life, it is already proof of the presence of
grace in our lives, a grace that flows unto us by means of those
mysterious junctures and connections of that most "astonishing
community," the Communion of Saints.

I would like to conclude this conference by quoting Dom
André Louf, who describes an experience he, as a Cistercian
monk, had during a visit to Mount Athos some years ago. In a
talk he once gave, he spoke of a visit with a hermit upon the
holy mountain:

> Suddenly, I was very, very touched by a deep impression
> that in this private chapel before a primitive iconostasis, in
> the sanctuary of this hermit I was really at the heart of the
> world and of the Church. There was nothing more impor-
> tant than to be there and pray. The only important thing in
> the world was to be there before the face of Christ.

This is the attitude a monk should have in the presence of
all that cries out to us for response. The only thing that matters
is to *be* there, in the monastery, at the heart of the world, at the
heart of the Church, and pray.

---

19. Georges Bernanos, *Les Prédestinés* (Paris: Éditions du Seuil, 1983) 99.

3

MISSA SINE NOMINE

If we were to seek the key to the authenticity of the spiritual journey, that key would perhaps be depth. "Becoming" is the essence of the spiritual journey. The movement of the journey is characterized by a dynamic transformation of being, in which "doing" is at the service of "becoming." In a sense, the traveller is the substance of the journey. *Being* connotes depth. A journey toward *spiritual being* depends on depth and is consequently a journey toward depth, within depth, and out of depth. Such a thought at once fascinates and mystifies us, for we really do not understand what depth is. Have we plumbed the depths of depth? Depth and *spiritual being* present us with more mysteries. Let us contemplate these mysteries with the aid of some images and symbols.

There is a sculpture by Henry Moore entitled "Mother and Child: Hollow." The *processus* of stone sculpture is very symbolic of the journey toward *spiritual being,* and this particular sculpture is a powerful visual image of that *processus.* The "mother" is a hollowed out form and the "child" a new life surging up within this hollow. Hollowness and birth; kenosis and new life: these are the essence of this journey. Looking deep into the hollow of this form, inhabited as it is by a new life, one sees the effect of *kenosis,* that emptying of self or the death which precedes all new life and rebirth. *Kenosis* is essential to the journey toward *spiritual being;* without it there is no depth, no transformation. The depth of our *spiritual being* somehow corresponds to the depth of our kenosis.

To return to the metaphor: in the *processus* of sculpting, *kenosis* is symbolized by the very act of sculpting—chipping away at the stone. This act is integral to the whole process because not only the figure that emerges along the way but also the stone being removed is part of the sculpture. This constant, inexorable chipping away with hammer and chisel witnesses to the passion behind the act. Transposed, it symbolizes the passion that is behind, the passion that motivates the *kenosis* integral to our spiritual "art." The more ardent the act of sculpting, the more intimately is the artist implicated in the medium. The closer the relationship between artist and art, the more fully will the sculptor draw substance from the work and become one with it. The art of sculpting is highly symbolic of the journey to *spiritual being*, characterized as it is by an underlying irresistibility which provides the impetus for the journey. We draw our substance progressively from an increasingly intimate *contact* with the spiritual realities we encounter, and ultimately we become one with the journey.

The journey to *spiritual being* is a *processus* of *kenosis* leading to new life: the paschal journey. Michelangelo, ardently engaged in sculpting one of his statues, is reputed to have said: "Another few days and life will break through."[1] This phrase echoes the hope of the spiritual journey: "another few days" of chipping away, of hollowing out, of emptying self, and *spiritual being* will break through! Inspired by this hope, we keep on journeying.

We know that this journey toward depth implies transformation and that the journey toward depth of *spiritual being* implies an ontological transformation. Such a *processus* can only unfold in the ground of our being, in our *heart*. Monastic spirituality teaches us that we must "return to the heart" *(reditus ad cor)*; this orientation can become the thrust of one's entire spiritual life. Certainly this path is not confined to the monastic life although it is connatural with it. Every person has the capacity to attain *spiritual being*; every Christian is called by baptism to participate in the fullness of *spiritual being* through the gift of

---

1. Irving Stone, *The Agony and the Ecstasy* (New York: New American Library, 1961) 394.

the Holy Spirit. For all of us, it is a long journey—the journey of a lifetime—for the spiritual life is essentially a process of continual, albeit imperceptible, transformation. This transformation can lead to the fullness of *spiritual being*, the outpouring of spiritual being which I call "spiritual priesthood": an ontological mediation, as it were, a mediation of a spiritual rather than a canonical order. Such a vision is as beautiful as it is awesome, as demanding to realize as it is difficult to understand.

There is a book to which I would like to refer as a means of helping us grasp what I am trying to say about *spiritual being*. It is *Missa sine Nomine*, written by Ernst Wiechert.[2] In and of itself, this book transmits something very beautiful—it could even be called sublime. Yet the context in which I am using it—to elucidate my vision of *spiritual being* and spiritual priesthood—is not necessarily in line with the author's intention.

Missa sine Nomine: the very title of the book captures the essence of transformation. According to the translator's note to the French edition, the meaning the title had for the author remains a mystery, for he died shortly after finishing the book. One of his friends, however, proposed as an explanation that Wiechert might have used it in a symbolic sense; just as in the Mass the mystery of transubstantiation unfolds, so the novel evokes a spiritual metamorphosis unfolding in the soul of a former inmate of a concentration camp. This is the story of his conversion and, through him, of those around him. *Missa sine nomine* would then symbolize the anonymous celebration of a spiritual renewal. For me, this title evokes an image of the hidden reality that occurs not in a church but within the heart of a human being: the celebration of the deepest mystery of our faith. Through the grace of God, this "spiritual priesthood" is accessible to everyone, but it is especially characteristic of the monastic vocation.

As both an aside and a prelude to something I intend to develop further along in this conference, I would like to stress

---

2. Ernst Wiechert, *Missa sine Nomine* (Erlenbach-Zürich: Rentsch, 1950). Translated by Marie Heynemann and Margery B. Ledward, *Tidings* (New York: Macmillan, 1959).

here that the book recounts the profound inner transformation of an individual and its repercussions on those around him; the *leitmotif* employed by the author to symbolize this subtle interior metamorphosis is the music of Mozart. This analogy I find an appropriate vehicle for explaining somewhat the intangible mystery of *spiritual being*. I will come back to this point after giving a summary of the story.

> Baron Amadeus, one of three brothers, returns from war to find that the château which had belonged to his family has now become the American headquarters. He goes directly to the sheepfold where his two brothers are living. Finding him profoundly distressed and in need of solitude, his brothers decide to move from the sheepfold and lodge nearby, leaving him alone to work through his trauma while remaining close enough to be able to visit him.
>
> Baron Amadeus had experienced war and captivity. He was devastated by what human beings had done to one another and by his own participation in that inhumanity. He has no hope, no love, and no future. The universe seems like stone, immobilized by years of horror. He has no love for humanity; he has lost faith in human beings. And his heart and mind feel as though they, too, have turned to stone. It is at this moment that he takes up his abode in the sheepfold. Even though he is alone, it seems to him that no solitude and no deprivation will be great enough to make him forget man's inhumanity to man. The screams of the tortured and the cries of the dying seem forever to have obliterated both the music of Mozart which once resounded in the château, and the voices of the peasants recounting their traditional tales.
>
> Nevertheless, Amadeus remains there, alone in the sheepfold, immersed in his own surroundings—spending hours near the fire, speaking with those who come to visit him and becoming part of their lives, taking long walks, living in harmony with nature, and, eventually, he becomes once again able to play the music of Mozart on his violoncello. Slowly, imperceptibly, a conversion and transformation have taken place in the heart of Amadeus and, through him, in the hearts of others. Because he continues to live in the sheepfold, his brothers offer to enlarge it for

him. He prefers, however, that it remain as it is, explaining
that "man does not need more space than a cell." Thus,
living in solitude, in a "cell," immersed in his own environment, Amadeus—through a deep inner transformation—ultimately becomes the celebrant of the "Missa sine
nomine."

Transposing this scenario to a specifically monastic context,
one sees the importance of immersion in the transformation of
being. Amadeus lived in solitude, in a cell, immersed in his own
surroundings. For the monk, conversion and transformation
take place in a monastery where one is immersed in the monastic
world. Within this *milieu*, the spiritual journey unfolds, rooted in
the Mystery of Christ. In *Missa sine Nomine*, conversion is presented as a metamorphosis, a passing from hatred to love and
from bitterness to charity. The fruit of this transformation is
spiritual being. The goal of our monastic journey is to one day
arrive at an outpouring of *spiritual being*, a state I refer to as
"spiritual priesthood," a state in which we ourselves become
the celebrants of a "Missa sine nomine" which is offered for the
salvation of the world.

I should perhaps reaffirm here that this deep conversion
and transformation are for the most part an unconscious process. Throughout *Missa sine Nomine* the seemingly banal phrase
"seated on the doorstep" recurs. This phrase is, in fact, rife with
meaning and significance, and heralds an ontological change in
the person who is described as "seated." For instance,

> Amadeus remained *seated on the doorstep* . . . For the first
> time, Amadeus thought that much had happened in this
> year . . . When he sat on the doorstep a year ago he had
> been different.[3]

Although the action remained the same: "seated on the
doorstep," the man's *being* had changed since the preceding
year. He suddenly realized that he was different, although he is
unable to define the exact nature of the dynamic involved in

3. Wiechert, *Tidings*, 137. Emphasis mine.

this change. Something similar can be true in our lives. We can remain in the same place, occupied with the same things—doing the same work, singing the same psalms, walking in the same cloister—year after year, and yet, through our immersion in the Mystery of Christ, our *being* is changing. This subtle and progressive conversion and transformation constitute the very soul and substance of our vocation. We are called to the monastery not to "do" something but to "become" someone, and the *spiritual being* resulting from this transformation is the goal of all our journeying. One could call it "sanctity," "divinization," or "spiritual priesthood," for all of these terms refer back to the ultimate mystery of the Christian vocation: "I live now . . . with the life of Christ who lives in me."

Permit me to share with you an excerpt from *Missa sine Nomine* that alludes to the supernatural beauty of the music of Mozart, a beauty that witnesses to the presence of something divine in humanity. In his youth Baron Amadeus had often played Mozart, but after the years of war and captivity he could no longer do so. He had, as was said, lost all belief in the nobility of humanity. His heart, now stone, was no longer capable of vibrating to the sublime melodies of Mozart. And yet one day, many years later, he found himself once again able to play Mozart's music. This symbolizes his inner transformation. Through a progressive conversion, his *heart* was born anew—it became capable of echoing the divine, connatural with the sublime. The following beautiful passage from the end of the book gives us an insight into what the music of Mozart revealed to Baron Amadeus about the deepest mystery of the human *heart*—something I refer to as the mystery of *spiritual being*.

> The "Ultimate" was the larghetto of the last piano concerto which Mozart had written. Amadeus had transcribed it for their three instruments. It was just a makeshift, but it had seemed to him as if something immortal remained immortal even when it was played on a linden leaf.
>
> For him it was the ultimate, the highest that a man whom God had inspired could attain. Or that a man who tried to commune with God could reach. Only he could write it

who thought that he saw the last sunset through the first shades of darkness, but in such a way that nevertheless the sun stood above the shadows. Only then had he left time behind him, all earthly time. Only then did he speak again as children speak. With the great simplicity in which word unites with word, and sentence fits sentence. With the freedom from fear of a child who feels quite safe and with the perfect happiness of that child. Without discord and untouched by the fall of man. Where the melody rises without effort like the fragrance from the cup of a flower, even without consciousness. As if it had always been there, but only now—in the evening of life—it rose, as the scent of the dame's violet rises sweetest in the evening.

Between these simple notes there sounded the promise that man was blessed after all. It was given not as a religious promise, but because a man had been able to write these notes, just these and no others. Because he might have written them down even in the darkest times—during a pestilence or during a religious war. Because all the powers were impotent before him who had heard these notes for the first time. Because it was unimportant what they were called—whether they were called unearthly or celestial notes. For these words only meant they had left earth and time behind them.

That's why it might be said that man was blessed, not only the especial being who had conceived this melody, but man in general, the whole of mankind. Because this lay within his sphere. Not only the curse of war and plague, not only murder and lies, or haughtiness and slander, but also this, this quiet, childlike dialogue with God—and that's why Amadeus called it the "ultimate."[4]

These words speak eloquently and powerfully to me of the human person's innate capacity for God, a gift that is given to us all and constitutes who we really are. The passage speaks to me of the infusion of this seed of divine life, of its diffusion within our *heart*, and of its effusion into the world through our

4. Ibid., 284–285.

transformed being. What seems to be especially portrayed here is its effusion *in the evening of life;* that is to say, upon the attainment of a certain spiritual maturity. The journey of conversion and transformation can ultimately bear fruit in the effusion of *spiritual being,* an effusion which is effortless, un-self-conscious and anonymous, like the scent of wine exhaled from a chalice or the perfume of dame's violet embalming the evening. This "effusion" *is* the celebration of the *Missa sine nomine.* It *is* the "spiritual priesthood."

In the closing lines of the excerpt, we read that once Mozart had heard the divine music within himself, not even the most horrendous events around him could prevent him from writing that music. Darkness could not obscure the light. In Baron Amadeus's own experience, something survived despite the pervasive evil that marked his years of war and captivity, something that could not be destroyed—we might call it the inner echo of a divine music. Once the divine has been born in us, has awakened in our *heart,* and has seized our *being,* no darkness can overcome it. The *Missa sine nomine* celebrated in the realm of *spiritual being* is unstoppable.

4

MUNDANE CULTURE—
HEART CULTURE

The contemplative and cenobitic dimensions of Cistercian life, the fundamental themes recently focused upon by our Order in General Chapters, capture the essence of the dynamics of the *heart*. To renew these two dimensions of our monastic life is to renew our *heart*, and to renew our *heart* is to renew these two dimensions of our monastic life. In signaling the need to reflect upon and rejuvenate these two aspects of our lifestyle, the Order, consciously or not, has set us firmly on the traditional monastic paths that lead to and flow from the deep *heart*. For what is contemplation but spiritual consciousness, and what is cenobitic life but charity, and what is the root of both realities but the *heart*?

With this "heart-vision" as a backdrop, allow me to share with you some reflections that were formulated in preparation for the General Chapters of 1993 and 1996. With a view to the Chapter of 1996, which focused on the cenobitic dimension of our lifestyle, I was asked to present a paper for discussion at our Regional Meeting on the question of providing an adequate formation to the cenobitic life in today's cultural context. I suppose that the assumption lurking behind the topic was that a more contemporary approach was now required to build and form community. Allow me to repeat these comments for you in the hope that, even if its content appears aimed specifically at those who are immediately involved in formation, it could be of interest to others. In actual fact, every one of us, whether "formers" or "formees," is implicated in formation, whether initial or ongoing, for it is a lifetime process in which we all must participate.

In my estimation, a formation in the cenobitic life which could be considered adequately related to our culture and times would not be all that different from what it has always been because, in essence, it all hinges on the question of "depth," which remains an invariable. Depth is the *sine qua non* for assimilation of values (itself the touchstone of formation), therefore any contemporary problems presenting critical challenges to the formation process, perhaps revolve around this primary consideration. Let us look more closely at the matter.

The simple fact that, as an Order, we have deemed it propitious to reflect upon such matters as the communal dimension of our life poses questions. Why this interest? Is it because we sense some urgent need for a more modern approach to community? Must we look outside to supplement our monastic tradition, to seek something that will provide adequate formation in community living? Or do we already, within the monastic tradition, possess abundant resources that would be more than sufficient for presenting this aspect of our spirituality to the new generation?

If the latter is the case and formidable difficulties exist despite our traditional resources, is this perhaps an indication that our communities are failing to incarnate this rich monastic vision in their existential reality? And why would that be? Could "individualism" be the worm eating away at the heart of the cenobium? No doubt it exists, and where it exists, it is the nemesis of community life. Yet, what is the root source of individualism? Could it be superficiality, a lack of immersion in monastic life that results in a lack of depth in the person of the monk, with direct repercussions on the tenor of community life? If so, whence comes this superficiality, this incapacity to immerse and engage oneself within the bounds of the monastic tradition? Evidently the causes are multiple, springing from the liabilities and limitations of both our human nature and personal histories, in addition to societal influences, which compound the whole.

Building a civilization, or simply a distinctive lifestyle, requires an interior culture and an interior vision—the outer shell must have an inner soul. Today, it is becoming increasingly difficult to transmit a monastic vision or culture because, in general, people seem to be more or less devoid of interiority, even in its most rudimentary forms. We live in a secularized civilization characterized by distractions. Curiosity, superficiality, and the pleasure principle dominate. We are thus assured of a state of somnolence where dullness and denseness reinforce the flight from self and the flight from God.

The interior vision or the inspiration at the core of such a civilization reveals itself to be radically individualistic, if not outright narcissistic. This orientation generates infrastructures marked by aggressive competition, materialism, unabated consumerism, and unconscionable exploitation. As the only valid point of reference, the individual has replaced both God and the community. The only absolute admitted into this void is absolute relativism, founded on a warped rendition of self-love.

In a society strongly influenced by the information revolution, by computer technology and media-glut, the world becomes smaller and smaller while, ironically, interpersonal relations are at a high risk of becoming rare, impersonal, and superficial. Overstimulated by the media, imagination and passions run amuck. Internet obsession offers more (and sometimes better) information, but does it offer more wisdom?

Group values are no longer assured by the family unit, the Church, or the state, insofar as these traditional institutions are themselves in the throes of crisis and mutation. Modern opportunities for experiencing community are often relegated to the realm of "self-help" support groups or, most unfortunately, to gangs, sects, and ethnic factions. It is often the case that interpersonal relationships are shaped by the narcissistic needs of the partners, each using the other to attain egotistical ends and self-affirmation. Commitment, sacrifice, and self-transcendence are rare gifts in a world where everything is disposable—people as well as things. And yet, emerging from within this secular frame of mind, we have a spiritual phenomenon labeled "New Age," which, despite its faddish trappings, is interpreted by some as being indicative of a spiritual awakening in our epoch and rooted in an authentic spiritual thirst.

This then is the "civilization" in which our monasteries, at least in the West, are implanted; this is the "culture" from which our candidates come. To the extent that our monastic culture continues to be impregnated with its traditional spirituality and our monastic communities remain capable of giving coherent expression of this interior vision, it is inevitable that some degree of traumatic tension is likely to erupt when these two worldviews meet in the formation process, whether initial or ongoing.

If one were to compare some of the dominant traits of these two divergent world visions, just to get a better sense of the potential tension, it would probably look something like this:

individualism affronting community
consumerism deriding simplicity
distraction high-jacking attention and vigilance
curiosity aborting assimilation
independence challenging obedience
narcissism negating self-sacrifice
hedonism scorning asceticism
the charismatic rejecting the institutional

Surely, the truth contains more nuance than a brief synopsis permits. Even so, this outline suggests that the transition from one culture to the other will require a considerable amount of time, and a great deal of patience, flexibility, and creativity on the part of everyone involved: the initiates, the formation team, the communities, and the Order.

In the light of this—undoubtedly too simplistic—analysis, which has focused on some of the more salient features of the dominant world culture, let us now return to the initial reflection regarding the relationship between depth and an adequate formation to cenobitic life.

To form community, one has to begin with individual members. To form the individuals, one must seek to reach into their depths. For this purpose, we have recourse to a spirituality aimed at awakening the *heart* to spiritual realities and to a spiritual world, and to do this through the progressive refining of the spiritual senses. This endeavor demands the cultivation of *spiritual being*. To facilitate an ever deeper personal immersion in the monastic "civilization," of which community life is an essential element, we try to unearth, in the *heart* of the individual, a certain correlation or affinity with monastic values. As Olivier Clément writes,

> The purpose of *ascesis* [I would say "monastic life"] is thus to divest oneself of surplus weight, of spiritual fat. It is to dissolve in the waters of baptism, in the water of tears, all the hardness of the heart, so that it may become an antenna of infinite sensitivity, infinitely vulnerable to the beauty of the world and to the sufferings of human beings, and to God who is Love . . .[1]

What a wonderful definition of the *heart:* an antenna of infinite sensitivity, vulnerable to beauty, to suffering, and to love! The deep *heart* is so alive, so sensitive, that to have access to this level of our *being* is tantamount to discovering a "sixth sense."

The *heart* is the "locus" of the spiritual life, the motor that powers our spiritual quest. The journey home is a journey of the *heart*. Monastic life is a finger pointing within, indicating the path that leads to the deepest center, to the true self: the path of *reditus ad cor*. When we return to the heart, we return to God. We return to "paradise" by an interior path; we return to ourselves; we claim the interior landscape of the *heart* as our own. Monastic life is essentially a process of awakening the dormant *heart*, liberating the life within, and following its lead.

It all seems so simple, so straightforward, so natural. Spiritual life should flow naturally because it is just that, *life*, a vital force within us waiting to be tapped, to become a well of living water, springing up into eternal life. Let us listen again to Olivier Clément:

1. Olivier Clément, *The Roots of Christian Mysticism*, translated by Theodore Berkeley and revised by Jeremy Hummerstone (London: New City, 1993) 131.

Ascesis [here I would say the "spiritual life"] is not obedience
to some abstract categorical imperative. It frees human
nature to follow its deep instinct to ascend towards God. It
enables a person to pass from a state "contrary to nature"
to a state "in harmony with nature" . . .[2]

To obey a vital interior dynamism. To follow our deepest
instinct. To recover our original harmony. To be consistent with
our true nature: this is the life of the *heart*, a life accessible to all.
And yet this is not our ordinary experience. Why is it so com-
plicated to be simple, so difficult to be natural? Why must one
calculate so hard just to *be?*

The biblical and theological response to these questions is
that we are wounded by sin and consequently alienated from
God and from our true nature, deformed as it is by our complicity with evil. The *heart*, the organ of *spiritual being,* has been
rendered more or less inoperative, dulled by the sediments of
sin encrusting its vitality. And so it is not just a matter of "returning to the heart" but of "recreating the heart," and only
Christ can assure us this new genesis, this new beginning, this
new *heart*. Placide Deseille puts it this way:

> It is crucial to understand that spiritual life is, essentially,
> *life of the heart recreated by grace,* obedience to a vital
> dynamism, and not just submission to an exterior law.[3]

The article on heart in the *Vocabulaire de Théologie Biblique*
alludes to the centrality of Christ and to the role of grace in the
restoration of the human *heart*. The *heart* is presented as the
center of the person, the place of intimate dialogue with oneself,
as well as the place where one opens oneself, or closes oneself, to
dialogue with God. The *heart* is the very source of our conscious,
intelligent, and free personality. It is the place of our decisive
choices, of the unwritten Law, of the mysterious action of God;
it is the privileged place of encounter with God, an encounter

2. Ibid., 132.
3. Placide Deseille, *L'Echelle de Jacob et la Vision de Dieu* (Aubazine:
Monastĕre la Transfiguration, 1974) 58.

which was fully actualized in the human *heart* of Jesus Christ. All of salvation history can be approached from the perspective of the *heart:* the human *heart* was created in the "image of God"; through sin, the original integrity of the *heart* has been compromised by turning away from its one true desire and seeking fulfillment in an array of idols. The paradigmatic journey of Israel from slavery to liberty is to be understood not only as a journey to the promised land but, more profoundly, as an interior journey toward the promise of a new *heart.* The Incarnation is the fulfillment of this promise, the restoration, in and through Christ, of the "image of God" which we are, with the concomitant hope of the divinization of the human *heart.* This fulfillment is the eternal design of God.[4]

Once again I am indebted to the insight of Olivier Clément, who refers to monasteries as "places for rebirth." It is a beautiful image and yet, like natural birth, the process implies great labor! To be born anew in Christ is the goal of monastic formation, both initial and ongoing. The womb to which we must return for this spiritual gestation is the *heart;* the inevitable labor pains stem from its purification, a purification effected by monastic *conversatio.*

I have nowhere found a more succinct and intuitive exposition of the spirituality of the *heart* than in the early writings of Placide Deseille, and so I will turn again to his teaching to help elucidate this subject. In an article regarding the "Jesus Prayer," he gives a concise description of the *heart* which expresses the essence of what I am trying to articulate. Deseille writes,

> The human heart, in the biblical sense of the word, designates this secret source whence proceeds [our] deepest spiritual life, made up, as it is, of all those spontaneous inclinations and the *"sens intime"*[5] of things that engage [our] very being. Through baptism, this heart is recreated by the Spirit, who engraves his Law upon it and penetrates it with his unction; in other words, there is inscribed

---

4. "Coeur," *Vocabulaire de Théologie Biblique,* edited by Xavier Léon-Dufour et al. (Paris: Editions du Cerf, 1970) 176–178.

5. Perhaps best translated as "deep-seated affinity."

within it a*n attraction for the good* which is capable of overcoming all the enticements of evil, and *a sense of God and his mysteries* by virtue of which the Christian should no longer have need of an exterior teaching, since this anointing teaches us all things (cf. 1 Jn 2:27). Yet, in actual fact, these divine energies dwell within us in a germinal state, requiring the cooperation (synergy) of grace and our free will in order to blossom into *a spontaneous orientation* of all the movements of our psyche towards God *(apathéia)*, as well as *an intuitive and savory experience of the divine presence* (contemplation, *théoria*). Besides, baptism permits other attractions to subsist within us; vestiges of sin, which grace gives us the power to combat but which nonetheless remain formidable obstacles.[6]

By this interpretation, the *heart* harbors an innate attraction for the law of God—a law of love—and a *sens intime* of spiritual realities that can mature into spiritual consciousness. This is equivalent to saying that the roots of charity and contemplation are firmly fixed in the *heart*. To awaken the *heart*, to purify the *heart*, or to unify the *heart* is to receive and bring to fruition the very gifts that God has implanted in our nature, offering us this grace and awaiting our assent and cooperation.

Again we see how beautiful, simple, and natural it all is. Yet, to return to our original reflection regarding contemporary culture, in the opinion of many, the dynamics inherent within that culture are not overtly propitious to the spiritual evolution of the human being. It is not surprising then that we find ourselves faced with a phenomenon of considerable amplitude: a more or less rampant spiritual insensitivity compounded by an equally rampant personal and psychological *hyper*sensitivity. Such a combination considerably complicates the task of formation and can have disastrous consequences on the tenor of community life as a "school of charity"—as the early Cistercians liked to call the monastery.

6. Placide Deseille, "La Prière de Jésus dans la Spiritualité Hésychaste," *Assemblées du Seigneur* 12 n.s. (1970): 64. Emphasis added.

Spiritual insensitivity is certainly not a new problem; one finds traces of it throughout all spiritual traditions. It is the consequence of a disordered state of soul, for which "purity of *heart*" is the proposed remedy. And yet one is tempted to say that, in this day and age, the carapace surrounding and dulling the spiritual sense has become even thicker. It is as if, in the prevailing materialistic, technological, and secular world culture, the spiritual dimension of our *being* has atrophied through systematic neglect.

With respect to the other aspect of the problem, *hyper*sensitivity, there we are dealing with an exaggerated emphasis on the individual's feelings and psychological sensitivities, an excess that can end in eclipsing the *sens intime* of spiritual realities which is so subtle to begin with. These egocentric psychological forces can be so pronounced as to compete with the dynamics of monastic formation, rendering them, for all intents and purposes, sterile.

All of this has direct repercussions on community life, which, for its cohesion, depends so much on the human and spiritual growth of its members and on their capacity for self-knowledge and transcendence through a continuing process of conversion. Individual persons, if they are too fragmented, may have considerable difficulty in achieving a healthy integration within the group. Interpersonal relations will be marked by varying degrees of dysfunctionality. It is as though the person's identity is so fragile and so tenuous that, just to be able to exist, it needs a barrage of defense mechanisms so deep-seated as to be almost second nature. If these defense mechanisms are too threatened by the challenges of community life, the person will either leave or become even more entrenched behind their blockades. The *hyper*sensitivity of such persons can render them almost incapable of evolving within the monastic context. They become, as it were, "untouchables." As a result, the community can come to resemble a constellation of more or less severely *blocked* members, paralyzed by their limitations. There is no question that limits are part of ordinary human existence; nevertheless, when they are too pervasive and too rigid to be altered in any constructive manner, a "school of charity" certainly faces challenges! I do not intend to insinuate by what has been said so far that "wounded-ness" renders a person unsuited to cenobitic life. Far from it! Our wounds can make us ever more permeable to grace, just as our supposed virtue can make us ever more impermeable to grace insofar as we feel no further need for it. In the final analysis, so much depends on the orientation of the person; individual reactions and responses are so unpredictable, a mystery.

So, where does all this leave us? What can we do to transmit monastic culture in these less than ideal conditions? Basically, our only recourse is to God. We must continually remind ourselves that, in this, as in every other instance, it is God who both takes the initiative and then upholds us in our efforts to awaken somnolent *hearts,* whether they are our own or those of others. It is by grace, and grace alone, that the dulled sensitivity of an anaesthetized *heart* can be reawakened and re-attuned to the summons of grace. And is this not another way of saying that "all is grace?"

The "antennas" of the *heart* are essentially receptors, not detectors. Before the ears of the *heart* can hear, God must first speak; God must shine forth if the eyes of the *heart* are to see. The *heart* senses God only when God "self-communicates." As Saint Augustine wrote,

> You called me; you cried aloud to me; you broke the barrier of my deafness. You shone upon me; your radiance enveloped me; you put my blindness to flight. You shed your fragrance about me; I drew breath and now I gasp for your sweet odour. I tasted you, and now I hunger and thirst for you. You touched me, and I am inflamed with love of your presence.[7]

Empowered by the certitude that God continues to take the initiative and self-communicate within and through monastic life—founded as it is upon the Mystery of Christ—I am convinced that this way of life can still be a viable bridge stretching

---

7. Saint Augustine, *Confessions*, Bk. 10. Translated by R. S. Pine-Coffin (London: Penguin Books, 1961, 1974) 232.

across the apparent abyss that separates mundane culture from a culture of the *heart*. What is called for today is what has always been called for—quite literally, an *in-depth* formation. Time, patience, flexibility, creativity, loving-kindness, and enlightened discernment are more necessary than ever before.

5

CONTEMPLATIVE IDENTITY
AND *LECTIO DIVINA*

I would like now to broach two intimately related topics: the contemplative dimension of monastic life and *lectio divina*. I will draw on materials presented at the General Chapter of 1993 and the Canadian Regional Conference that preceded it. If you are not yet weary of the terms: *immersion, depth,* and *being,* you will surely be after this conference!

Cistercian contemplative identity, as I understand it, emanates from what I refer to as an "immersion in the Mystery of Christ," effected within a monastic context. I have already alluded to the presence of this Mystery at the very core of our monastic way of life, a presence that makes possible an immersion of the substance of the person in the substance of the Mystery. To the degree that we live our lives immersed in the Mystery, this contact nourishes the fullness of the life of the Spirit sown in our *heart* at baptism. With the blossoming of the life of grace comes a certain *sens intime* of spiritual realities, the seed of contemplation.

Thus it is that when I reflect upon Cistercian contemplative identity, I perceive a vital relationship between immersion and contemplation. In addition, this concept speaks to me of *spiritual being* and its relationship to depth. Immersion and contemplation, depth and *being,* are all related. Immersion in the depths of the Mystery gives birth to *spiritual being,* which is the ground of contemplative identity. It is so simple. The dynamic is none other than the aforementioned "return to the *heart*": that spiritual practice which summons us to penetrate ever more deeply into the recesses of our *being* and into the intimate realities of the

Mystery of Christ in which we are immersed. A phrase from Psalm 42, "deep calls unto deep," admirably depicts this contemplative path: the mystery calls to the *heart*. Involved here are the depth both of the way of life and of the person living it.

What exactly is meant by "depth." Once again we are faced with a mystery to ponder, not a problem to solve. One could say that depth haunts us; we are drawn toward depth and within depth, because instinctively, intuitively, we sense that the meaning of our life is to be found there. When depths awaken, *spiritual consciousness* grows, *spiritual being* is born.

The door to depth will vary according to the person seeking to enter. What matters is that we are journeying toward depth: the depth of our own *being* and of the monastic life. Cistercian *life* must become Cistercian *experience* for Cistercian *identity* to emerge. This happens within the context of a spiritual journey into depths, a journey of and through depths that transforms the very *being* of the voyager. What I am referring to here is an ontological transformation, a *processus* that can take place only at the level of *being*, at the level of the *heart*. It is a long journey, the journey of a lifetime.

For the Cistercian, *transformation of being* occurs through an immersion in the ordinary, elemental daily routine of the monastic life. A very powerful spiritual force is present and acting in all the aspects of a lifestyle unified by the primacy of the spiritual. Cistercian monastic life plumbs great depths. Immersed in this life, given certain preliminary conditions of which I will speak, we are immersed in a spiritual reality that is capable of transforming us at the very core of our *being*. Monastic life in its totality and its integrity draws us ever deeper into the Mystery. All aspects of this life are intertwined and bound together, harmoniously and dynamically, orienting us toward one single goal: union with Christ. Immersion opens us to interpenetration, transformation, and divinization. It is through immersion in all the elements inherent in this lifestyle that we are immersed in the life of Christ, and it is by virtue of this immersion that what we have been calling our "Cistercian contemplative identity" is born. For the Cistercian monk, this identity is nothing other than becoming a living echo of Christ.

Though I am speaking in terms of experience and transformation, I do not mean to give the impression that our journey toward depth within the context of Cistercian life is a highly conscious process, even less a *self*-conscious process. It is, on the contrary, a more or less unconscious process. The utter ordinariness of our style of life, the subtlety of the workings of grace in us, and the sobriety and simplicity of our spirituality do not lend themselves to a purely human assessment of "progress" in the spiritual life. This subtle, gradual transformation unfolding at a level beyond our ordinary consciousness, is the very soul and substance of our vocation. At the same time, it can also become the source of temptation.

If we have the profound conviction that Christ, that the Mystery of Christ, is present and acting within the monastic vocation, we will be motivated to open ourselves more and more fully to what it asks of us. As a result, immersion will deepen, facilitating transformation. Without such a conviction, without this kind of faith, we may perhaps be tempted to fill apparent voids in this lifestyle with activities positive in and of themselves but which could finish by compromising the integrity of the elemental quality which is a characteristic of monastic life. As a result, the spiritual dynamic at work within the monastic context would then be vitiated. We could, for example, become impatient with the slowness of change, with the monotony of the journey, with the sobriety of the experience. We might then attempt to accelerate or animate everyday life with frills that are foreign to the authenticity of the Cistercian calling. As a consequence, we could be jeopardizing the germination of the seeds of *spiritual being* buried in the depths of our *heart,* seeds awaiting God's time for fruition. The possible result could be that our immersion, inevitably lacking in depth, would be compromised and rendered ineffective, and would contribute little or nothing to the growth of a Cistercian contemplative identity.

The Cistercian experience is characterized by a *processus* of transformation-by-immersion, which, although unconscious, is capable of liberating a new level of consciousness: a *heart* consciousness. As our *being* is imperceptibly transformed, so too is our *spiritual consciousness*. We begin to see things differently, feel things differently, and know things differently, because the eyes of the *heart*, the ears of the *heart*, and the intelligence of the *heart* have been opened. A new identity is being born, subtly emerging from the depths of our journey. This nascent *spiritual being*, and concomitant *spiritual consciousness, is* our Cistercian contemplative identity—an identity so sober and interwoven with the very fibers of our *being* that it emanates anonymously from our *heart* and pervades every aspect of our existence. One could almost call it *"contemplatio sine nomine."*

Thomas Merton grasped something of this quality of being in a reflection inspired by a passage in which Saint Paulinus used the phrase *resonare Christum*—"to resonate Christ." In Merton's words:

> These words *[resonare Christum]* sum up whole monastic life. Like a sea-shell, the monk, quiet and unobserved, possesses an unsuspected secret. He is altogether silent, like a shell on the table. But when we approach him and know him well, we hear the sound of waves breaking on the shores of heaven.[1]

I imagine you have all had the experience to which Merton alludes, of holding a seashell to your ear and seeming to hear an echo of the ocean. Yet, beyond that image, these words speak to me of contemplation and spiritual depth, both of which are needed in order to "resonate Christ"—which is, in essence, the goal of our Cistercian monastic journey.

Jean Guitton, a French philosopher and academician, once remarked that we can only really hear what resonates within us. For something to resonate within us, we need to have both depth and interior space as well as the capacity for receiving and perceiving. Monastic life makes some rather radical demands for arriving at this ontological attunement, at this refinement of *being* which emanates from depth and leads to ever greater depth: *kenosis,* porousness, continuity, duration, and openness. These are vital components of immersion, which in and of itself implies depth.

1. Thomas Merton, *Liturgy OCSO* 24.1 (1991) 10.

Let me go back to Merton's image of the seashell. The shell is *immersed* in the *depths* of the ocean; the water envelops it, the waves *penetrate* its *inner recesses* and, with time, it becomes united with, identified with, and, we could almost say, *one* with the ocean. Ultimately it comes to harbor within itself an echo of the ocean. The seashell is now a "carrier" of the ocean, and when we put it to our ear, we can hear it resonating the reality that, in a manner of speaking, it has *assimilated* by means of its *immersion*.

Let us retrace this metaphorical journey to depth. The seashell is immersed in an environment (experience), for a long time (duration); it remains there (continuity), receptive to (openness/porosity) a more intimate contact within its inner recesses (hollowed out by *kenosis*). In virtue of this *processus*, the seashell is transformed into an echo and carrier of the reality in which it is immersed.

To transpose the image to a higher plane, we can say that the monk is immersed in the Mystery of Christ by insertion into the Cistercian monastic life. All the exigencies of immersion that I have just mentioned are present, and they facilitate the penetration and inhabitation of the interior spaces of the *heart* by the Mystery which henceforth resonates within. "Contemplative identity" is formed by this *processus;* the monk becomes, so to speak, a "carrier" of the mystery.

I would now like to consider *lectio divina,* for it is a privileged means for attaining the contemplative dimension of monastic life and of nourishing the contemplative identity of the monk.

If one looks closely at *lectio divina,* one sees a sort of condensation of the contemplative dynamic inherent in our whole lifestyle. *Lectio* is a paradigm of immersion. It is a potentially dense and intense immersion because it is an immersion in the Word of God. It is an immersion of the person in the Word that carries the Mystery. An interpenetration of substances can take place by means of this immersion; the Mystery contained in the Word penetrates the *heart,* and the *heart* penetrates the Mystery. This dynamic of immersion and interpenetration is the essence of both *lectio divina* and contemplative life.

By its very nature, traditional *lectio divina* is a contemplative process which can lead us to a contemplative experience—to a union with the Mystery contemplated. Its contemplative nature should be respected. *Lectio* is *a way of being* with the Word, a process that requires a specifically contemplative attitude, a mode of being rather than *doing*. What it asks is simply that we *be present* and let the Word, the Mystery, come to us. This attitude disposes us to be "seized" or "conquered" by the Word instead of putting obstacles in its path by trying to grasp or conquer it!

Lectio divina, by putting us in contact with the Word, acts as a catalyst that stimulates within us the life of the Spirit. If we are truly receptive, *lectio* has the potential to connect or to attach us to the Mystery present in the Word; it is a conduit through which the Mystery can enter our *heart*. Through our immersion in the Word, *lectio divina* can render the Mystery present to us and can render us present to the Mystery. The progressive entry into the Mystery through the practice of *lectio*, as through the other aspects of our monastic life, can lead us, by the grace of God, to transformation and divinization, which is just another way of saying contemplation and union with God.

Recently I came across a book by Alphonse de Chateaubriant entitled *La Réponse du Seigneur*. In it I found a poem by Henrich Heine and a commentary by Chateaubriant.[2] I would like to quote both in reference to what I have just said about *lectio divina*. The poet is writing about a dream in which he finds himself drawn to the beauty of exquisite flowers that are out of his reach. Pining away, he implores a friend to build him a bridge so that he can get to them.

> I see in a dream marvelous flowers
> whose scent pierces me with languor and desire.
> From these flowers I am separated
> by an unfathomable abyss
> And my heart aches until it bleeds . . .

2. Alphonse de Chateaubriant, *La Réponse du Seigneur* (Paris: Grasset, 1933) 229–230.

Oh! these flowers! how they draw me,
how they glisten, alas!
Master Arlequin, my friend, could you not
build me a bridge?

Chateaubriant reacted to this poem by saying that he knows a better way to get to these flowers than a bridge: the connection of contemplation. He writes:

Master Arlequin, my friend, I have no need of your
scaffolding . . .
And no poet worthy of the name would ever again
have recourse to your bridge.
For I have found a better pathway, my friend,
I have contemplated these flowers.
Contemplated, you understand, contemplated . . .
contemplated . . . !

I contemplated them all day,
I contemplated them all night,
I contemplated them day and night,
Until one morning, at dawn, I opened my eyes,
And they were in my hand, my friend,
shimmering with dew.

Let us consider these lines and their relationship to *lectio divina*. If I modify them a bit and replace "flowers" with "Word" and "contemplate" with "'immersed," the Word would become the attraction and immersion the preferred means of making contact. The revised response would read:

. . . my friend, I have no need of your scaffolding . . .
For I have found a better pathway, my friend,
I have immersed myself in the Word.
Immersed, you understand, immersed . . .
immersed . . . !
Immersed in it all daylong,
Immersed in it all nightlong,
Immersed in it day and night,
Until one morning, at dawn, I opened my eyes,
And the Mystery contained in the Word was there in
my *heart*. . . .

Contemplation, immersion, depth—these bring us into contact with the reality to which our path leads. Our temptation—like the poet's— would be to want to construct "bridges," to attempt to grasp the Mystery through our own ingenuity. *Lectio divina* is an immersion in the Word, day and night. It is not a bridge that must be built. It is a pure *movement into* the Mystery, requiring a simplicity of approach that renounces this temptation to hurdle the abyss by man-made means, whatever they may be. This is equally true of the whole of our monastic life. The radical simplicity that characterizes *lectio* has its roots in the elemental bedrock of Cistercian spirituality.

Perhaps one of the greatest obstacles to the traditional practice of *lectio divina* is the manner in which it impoverishes us: it makes us feel inadequate, impotent. This is true, I suppose, of monastic life in general. It is a life as humble as the seashell on the table and yet it can lead us to the ultimate reality if we accept the inherent poverty of the process, trying neither to embellish it nor to give in to the ever-present temptation to construct bridges at every turn.

Lectio divina is a fundamental monastic practice. By its inexhaustible possibility of bringing us into contact with the Mystery of Christ through the Word, it forms the monk, and the monk forms the community. *Lectio* is a door to the contemplative dimension of our life, and therefore the contemplative dimension of that life—for both the individual and the community—depends on *lectio divina;* it is not an isolated monastic value. *Lectio* has an enormous influence on the tenor and integrity of our monastic life. Each and every effort to revivify this practice is, directly or indirectly, a step toward the deepening of the contemplative dimension of Cistercian life.

6

IN CONTACT WITH THE ELEMENTAL— ABSORBED BY THE DIVINE

Now I would like to draw your attention to a concept to which I have already alluded but which I now intend to expound upon: the notion of the "elemental."

"Elemental," as I understand it, means "reduced to the essential." It is a rudimentary state, a condition that accentuates the fundamental components or principles of a given reality. The elemental refers to the origins, the ground, the constitutive qualities of something. One might say that the elemental is like a space, an atmosphere, or a quality of being that yields itself to the essential, where everything is subordinated to and oriented toward the emergence of what is essential. The elemental, thus understood, becomes a "carrier" or an epiphany of the essential. All of this suggests that an elemental condition or state favors the emergence and the experience of the essential. The essential, in its turn, designates the primary, the vital, the indispensable, and the necessary. The essential is the irreducible truth of a reality; its authentic identity and *raison d'être*.

Because our Cistercian monastic spirituality is, unequivocally, an elemental spirituality in which everything is oriented toward the essential, we are already familiar with what the elemental would look like in the spiritual realm. Every aspect of our *conversatio* is profoundly in harmony with its underlying spirituality. The simplicity of Cistercian life, which is centered on the essential and enveloped by the elemental, both kneads our person and challenges our options. What is elemental is not just the lifestyle, inspired and governed by the principle of honoring the necessary while shunning the superfluous. The architecture and environment in which we are plunged day and night also exude the elemental. Immersion in this elemental matrix forges an elemental *being* which is capable of entering simply and spontaneously into contact with and mediating the essential.

Saint Benedict in his Rule defines the monk as someone who "truly seeks God," which is another way of saying that a monk is someone who truly seeks "the essential." Is this not also the ultimate goal of monastic life John Cassian describes in his First Conference?[1] What he refers to as the "Kingdom of God," comprised of "union with God" and "eternal life," could also be called the essential. Cassian is careful to note, however, that before anyone can arrive at this ultimate goal *(telos)*, there is a preliminary criterion, which he refers to as the immediate goal *(scopos)* of monastic life: "purity of heart." I take purity of heart to mean the return to an integral quality of *being*, unalloyed, wherein the deep *heart* has been purified like gold in the fire, which is akin to an elemental state of being. Understood this way, the ultimate goal of monastic life would be to usher the monk toward an encounter with the Essential. This goal is facilitated by the impulsion of an interior dynamism, which emanates from a pure, elemental *heart* that has recaptured and reidentified with its primitive aspiration: the irrepressible *élan*, impulse, toward the "one thing necessary."

I do not intend to give the impression that elemental being is the privileged domain of monastic life; it is characteristic of every Christian life that is lived profoundly. Perhaps the best example of this state of *being* is Mary, the Mother of God. Dare I suggest, in the light of this approach, that the mystery of the Immaculate Conception could be envisioned as the gift of original grace, regenerating human nature to its primitive state of purity and openness to the divine? It suggests that God had to ensure the existence of an elemental condition within the

---

1. John Cassian, "First Conference: On the Goal of the Monk," in *The Conferences,* translated by Boniface Ramsey, Ancient Christian Writers Series 57 (New York: Paulist Press, 1985) 35–75.

created order so that the " Essential" could surge forth from the flesh and blood of our human nature. I am reminded of a mosaic embedded in the sanctuary wall of our church. It is modeled after the "Virgin of the Sign"—sometimes called the "Virgin Orant." She stands there erect, simple, solitary, real, authentic— *elemental* in aspect—hands raised in prayer without artifice. And surging from her *heart*, from her womb, from her center is the Essential *par excellence*, the person of Emmanuel, God-with-us, Jesus Christ. She facilitated the emergence of the divine into the very heart of creation not only by her *fiat* but also by the quality of her *being*. It seems to me that there is an affinity be-tween the elemental and the divine, and the Virgin of the Sign icon has become a powerful image of this mysterious and inti-mate relationship.

Admittedly, this relationship between the elemental and the divine has fascinated me for some time, but recently I was stirred by a sudden impression. Someone had given me a small hand-carved wooden statue made in Haiti of a woman in prayer. She is poorly dressed, immobile, recollected, and elemental in aspect. I positioned the statue on my desk, next to the stone I mentioned earlier, the one whose ordinary exterior appear-ance harbors small crystals. At that moment came the impres-sion, an intuition captured by a few simple words: "in contact with the elemental, absorbed by the divine." It was then that I understood that the elemental and the divine are bound!

The awareness of this mysterious liaison reminds me of what I learned some years before entering the monastery by reading Georges Bernanos. I first knew of him through the media, and later more intimately through his novels. His writ-ings sensitized me to the elemental character of spirituality, for the elemental was always present in the supernatural overtones inherent in his works. Immersed as I was in these books, I was captivated, though somewhat unconsciously, by this rapport between the elemental and the supernatural.

Bernanos had an acute sense of what we call "sanctity." He understood it to be a supernatural *ontological* reality. His "saints" are surrounded by an elemental atmosphere and their very per-son, their very *being*, is elemental. In his novels, the characters closest to sanctity are notably unsuccessful in life, rather awkward, indigent, and far from mundane. They are, unbeknownst to themselves, quite simply channels of grace for others. Through these characters Bernanos attempts to convey what was, for him, the essence of sanctity. His "saints" are portrayed as receptacles of the divine. His narratives relating to the supernatural are quite remarkable and, to a degree, embody what I mean when I allude to the existence of *another order* in the spiritual life.

In 1968, I received a letter from a friend of Bernanos, Irénée Valéry-Radot, who had entered the monastery of Bricquebec. I must have written to him requesting some information regarding Bernanos. Some of the details in his letter confirmed a conviction dear to Bernanos that a priest worthy of the ministry of grace had to be *a priori* an "elemental" person, empty of self and given to God. I quote here from the letter in which he wrote of Bernanos' death:

> Father Pézeril is the priest who brought communion to Bernanos every morning, coming all the way in from his parish of Saint-Séverin, where he was vicar, to the American hospital at Neuilly, and this because Bernanos had refused to see the resident chaplain, whom he deemed too worldly . . . For five months he made this trip and it was he who attended to Bernanos in his final agony on July 5, 1948.

Over the years my intuition that a connection exists between the elemental and the divine has become a conviction. It now appears to me that there is a veritable connaturality between the elemental and the divine. I sense a similar insight in the thought of Simone Weil. In a reflection on her ideas on the Eucharist, Jean Guitton stated:

> It is a question of taking what is lowest on the ladder of beings, a fragment of matter (in this case a fragment of bread), and saying that this fragment of bread truly contains the divine infinity represented by the God-man Christ, come to bring salvation to humanity. Is there not between the first term—that is to say, the fragment of matter—and the second term—that is to say, the divinity—such a

distance that to say that one *is* the other is an absurdity?
But it is here that the thought of Simone Weil is original.
For her, what I call matter, which is the lowest degree of
Creation, is precisely the receptacle most worthy of the
divinity. Simone Weil often indicated (quite different in
her views from those of Teilhard de Chardin) that, beyond
animality, there is "vegetality," but beyond the vegetal, she
places the mineral, and probably the crystal, and probably
the host. We are here at the lowest degree of Creation, but
it is just this degree, by virtue of its being the lowest, that is
the most capable of receiving the infinite. There was, for
her, a connaturality between a fragment of matter and the
infinite . . . Between things that occupy the most distant
properties, there exists, for those who look deeply, an
affinity.[2]

The elemental and the divine. A fascinating mystery. The
lowest attracting the highest, the least seized by the most, becoming a receptacle of grace. It makes me think of the *anawim*,
the poor in spirit, and of all those spoken of in the Beatitudes
who hunger for the Absolute, are pure of heart, meek, merciful,
persecuted, afflicted—human beings who, having been reduced
to the essential, inherit the Kingdom, share in divine life, and
for whom "to live is Christ!" The elemental can be understood
as a nakedness, an indigence disclosing a vital need for fulfillment, a fulfillment that is humanly unachievable without the
divine. The Beatitudes unveil for us this paradox of a sanctity
that blossoms from within a human starkness, which one could
call an elemental sanctity.

Christian holiness signifies neither the perfecting of self
nor the acquisition of virtues. In fact, the "self" can never attain
sanctity; it is beyond the realm of human possibilities. One
could rightly say that sanctity is not of this world. Sanctity is of
another order, one which human means can never attain. The
human alone can neither grasp nor imitate it; on a purely
human scale, sanctity is not even discernable! And yet, despite

2. Jean Guitton, *L'Absurde et le Mystère* (Paris: Desclée de Brouwer, 1984) 99.

all this and as improbable as it may seem, it is precisely to this *other order* that we are called.

The road leading to this *other order* is elemental, implying kenosis and divestment of all that is superfluous and peripheral. I am here reminded of Jules Monchanin's description of his spiritual journey in India. One can sense through his words the radicality and asperity inherent in the uncompromising path of an elemental spirituality.

> Detachment, breaking off, renunciation. Harshness, too, and monotony of weeks, months, years without change. The relentless call of God has left only the taste for the essential and the essential is concealed. . . . If there are joys, a secret urgency recalls that they must be crossed over. . . . There is only exodus and no *extasis* . . . Yet, exodus has no meaning except through the Promised Land, and this absence is the reverse and the annunciation of the Presence.[3]

Elsewhere he writes:

> Endless walking across the unchanging plains of alpha, rock, and sand, where mirages vanish. . . . Desert patience of one who is called . . . to a vision which will make him forget all things previously seen. Harshness, severity of forms and lines. The accidental is worn away by the essential: God is sufficient.[4]

Certainly, it is not necessary to travel to India or literally to inhabit a desert to experience the irresistible attraction of the divine call; what is requisite is to enter into contact with the deepest truth of our *being*. Listening to it, we will be seduced by it. We must re-become who we *are* before becoming who we are called to *be*, both under the auspices of God's grace. Each of us

---

3. Jules Monchanin, *In Quest of the Absolute,* edited and translated by J. G. Weber. Cistercian Studies Series 51 (Kalamazoo, MI: Cistercian Publications, 1977) 169.
4. Ibid., 168.

is *capax Dei*—"capable of God"; it is our most elemental state. We are called to "become God" (as some Church Fathers dared to put it). We are earthen jars capable of becoming repositories of the divine. This is the essential.

It is all so extraordinary, so unexpected. We must never take for granted this awesome mystery of our *being* in-relation-with *Being*. There is always a risk that we will let this remain at a conceptual, doctrinal, dogmatic level. No, it must become "experience" and it is the elemental that, in a certain manner, "channels" that experience. There is a quality, inherent to the elemental, that haunts, mystifies, seduces, and attracts us. I believe that this intangible quality flows from its connaturality and affinity with the divine. Truly to be in contact with the elemental can lead to "absorption," so to speak, by the Divine.

I am reminded of a reflection written by a postulant some years back. The community was viewing an audio-visual presentation on contemplative life, and there was background music. The "active" attention of this woman was centered on the slide show, but the ears of her *heart* were listening to the music. Suddenly, the elemental quality of the music of the panflute awoke in her profound spiritual sentiments; it was as if, catalyzed by the sound of the flute, she had momentarily been "absorbed" by the Mystery. Her words eloquently recount the experience:

> Sometimes we wonder what has happened to us that we have suddenly become aware of something that had always been present, only we never noticed it before. What we then see, hear, or feel is absolutely new, unmistakably real, and very powerful.

> When I listened that night to Dvorak's second movement of The New World Symphony, I was moved, as always, by this bitter-sweet composition. As always, I became more closely fused with the sense of darkness that is inherent in being human. Filled with such sentiments, I did not immediately notice the transition to a new piece of music. Suddenly, I woke up, or rather something deep inside of me awoke upon hearing the sound of the panflute.

The purity of the sound was like light and illuminated all—"suddenly in a shaft of sunlight. . . ." The sound was more than pure, it was piercing, incisive . . . indeed it penetrated my whole being like a blade, leaving a spacious wound. The pain began to rise out of a never felt part of me; it rose in small ripples and spirals, growing ever more intense as it filled all of me, never leaving the center of my existence. Tears welled up in my eyes, in response to the searing wound that burned like a powerful flame.

The haunting beauty of the flute called to the deep within me and wakened Babylon's strangeness and the anguished cry of one who is far from home. The languishing sound seemed to wail for a return to the soil it grew in. And I, too, was suddenly aware of what feeling was being produced in me: *Heimweh,* the longing for home. Intense recollection and knowledge of this sound, yet never heard before. It is part of me, and I am part of its infinite sound, for there seems to be no discernable beginning or end to its presence. The longer I listened, the more I felt a sense of agelessness, and of "all is always now."

A primordial sound, *Urton,* hollow sphere, the wood of which must have grown in Eden. It grew in soil that is foreign to us now, but our roots being there, our longing, too, is rooted there. Never therefore shall we rest, shall we be able to rest until we are home once again. Perhaps here lies the key to all the restlessness and aching longing, the never ending search for that which is most deeply our own. Perhaps we ought not to look for "home" in our present world, for I sense it cannot be found. It is the human being's destiny to be homeless, yet always homeward bound—a nomad, a traveler, *homo viator.*

The panflute reminds me of the faraway high places in such a way that the sound fuses the center of my existence with all that was and all that will be. The flute stands before me, a messenger, an image, an icon; the hollow spheres carry no other mark, the sound depends on perfect control of the lips and breath. Like a word that is formed on our lips as we become aware of its meaning. It is not only wind or air but fire soaring through its body. It

is a burning flute, creating a flaming song. It does not offer
itself as medium only. It is medium and offering; it is sacrifice.[5]

The panflute is elemental in form—a space that offers itself
as carrier of the essential. The "primordial sound" that emanates from it is also elemental. The sentiment or experience
triggered in this woman was one of nostalgia and homesick-
ness. Obviously, this is the personal experience of one individual, but I suspect that it is universal in its essence.

Each of us is *capax Dei.* We are made for God. Our *being* is
radically incomplete and aspires to fulfillment. This is our most
elemental state or condition, and the deepest truth of our nature.
The elemental around us can facilitate the experience of the elemental within us, and, given this mysterious bond between the
elemental and the divine, contact with one *can* lead to absorption by the other. Herein lies the *raison d'être* of our elemental
monastic life.

Let us allow Blaise Pascal to bring this conference to a con-
clusion:

> What else does this craving, and this helplessness, pro-
> claim but that there was once in man a true happiness, of
> which all that now remains is the empty print and trace?
> This he tries in vain to fill with everything around him,
> seeking in things that are not there the help he cannot find
> in those that are, though none can help, since this infinite
> abyss can be filled only with an infinite and immutable
> object; in other words by God himself.[6]

---

5. Annette Vatter.
6. Blaise Pascal, *Pensées* (Paris: Éditions du Seuil, 1962) 148. Translated by
A. J. Krailsheimer (London: Penguin Books, 1966, 1973) 75.

7

IF YOU ONLY KNEW
WHAT GOD IS OFFERING
Babette's Feast[1]

The Word was made flesh and lived among us . . . full of
grace and truth. Indeed, from his fullness we have, all of
us, received—grace upon grace, since, though the Law was
given through Moses, grace and truth have come through
Jesus Christ. (Jn 1: 14, 16-17)

. . . there was a wedding at Cana in Galilee . . . the
mother of Jesus said to him: "They have no wine. . . ."
Jesus said to the servants: "Fill the jars with water. . . .
Draw some out now," he told them. (Jn 2:1a, 4, 7-8)

. . . Jesus, tired by the journey, sat down by the well. . . .
When a Samaritan woman came to draw water, Jesus said
to her: ". . . If you only knew what God is offering . . .
you would have been the one to ask, and he would have
given you living water. . . . Whoever drinks this water
will get thirsty again; but anyone who drinks the water
that I shall give will never be thirsty again: the water that
I shall give will turn into a spring inside him, welling up to
eternal life." (Jn 4: 6, 7, 10, 13-14)

Jesus answered: "I am the bread of life. He who comes to
me will never be hungry; he who believes in me will never

---

1. *Babette's Feast*, A film adaptation by Gabriel Arel of the novel by Isak
Dinesen. A Panorama Film, 1987.

thirst . . . and the bread that I shall give is my flesh, for the life of the world. . . . He who eats my flesh and drinks my blood lives in me and I live in him." (Jn 6:35, 51, 56)

On the last day and the greatest day of the festival, Jesus stood there and cried out: "If any man is thirsty, let him come to me! Let the man come and drink, who believes in me." As Scripture says: From his breast shall flow fountains of living water. He was speaking of the Spirit which those who believed in him were to receive . . . (Jn 7:37-39)

I have come so that they may have life and have it to the full. (Jn 10:10)

When they came to Jesus, they found he was already dead, and so . . . one of the soldiers pierced his side with a lance; and immediately there came out blood and water. (Jn 19:34, 35)

The grace of God. New wine. The gift of God. Living water. The bread of life. Fountains of living water. Life in abundance, grace upon grace: all this is what *Babette's Feast* signifies for me. What God wants to give us, what God has given us in Jesus: this is what *Babette's Feast* represents to me. The Eucharist, the messianic banquet, the feast of the Lamb, the eternal wedding celebration: this is what Babette's feast portrays for me. However, what *Babette's Feast* symbolizes above all else is that *other order* of which I spoke at the outset. *Babette's Feast* is my "secret!" In it is revealed ". . . the things that no eye has seen nor ear has heard, things beyond the mind of man, all that God has prepared for those who love him" (1 Cor 2:9). Babette's feast is our contact with and participation in divine life. It is the plentitude of *spiritual being,* a transformation that takes place at the level of the *heart,* and the life of the Beatitudes. It is also gratuitous gift of self, a holocaust, oblation, *kenosis.* All is there and *all is grace!* To see how I arrived at this, let us now reflect upon the film, which reconstructs Isak Dinesen's novel *Babette's Feast.* And what a deceptively simple tale it is, more parable than drama: an encounter between two worlds, two religions, and two visions of life.

The characters move about with apparent resignation well within the confines of their destinies, each tragic in its unique yet intertwined way. The storyline, like the dialogue, is sparse, but the very restraint inherent in the exposition underscores a richness of pathos and irony. A brief synopsis may help situate us:

"Once upon a time," there lived a pious family consisting of two daughters and a father who was the Protestant minister of a tiny sect of aging followers dwelling in a remote fishing village in Denmark. The lives of these two young women, totally controlled by their austere father, consisted of serving him, *his* God, and *his* flock. And yet, they seemed reconciled to their lot, knowing nothing more and expecting nothing more. Fate, however, had other designs, and the appearance of two most unlikely visitors risked awakening the sisters' deep-seated desires for the fullness of life and love. First, there was the young army officer whose heart stirred with noble yearning at the sight of the beauty and grace of the elder sister. Next, there arrived a famous tenor who, in the pure, angelic voice of the other sister, discerned the rare gift of a diva and therefore earnestly sought to foster her talent. Hope soared in the hearts of all these young people, but their bright futures were sabotaged by the wiles of the domineering minister who betrayed his daughters' joy on the sacrificial altar of his rigid, puritanical religion. Thwarted, the suitors departed, dejected and disheartened; the sisters acquiesced to the will of their father and consecrated the rest of their lives to the drudgery of a lifeless religion. They even carried on this obscure ministry after the death of their father, having so identified with his dead-end path that they had all but forgotten the promising horizons that once stretched out before them.

Many long, lonely years of toil and dedication passed in this way, wrapped in the sincerity of good deeds and selflessness but bearing little fruit in the hearts of the congregation, awash as it was in interpersonal bickering, back-stabbing, and bitterness. Grace slipped in unnoticed, however, in the guise of a widowed French Catholic woman, exiled from her strife-torn homeland and entrusted to the care of the sisters by the long-gone opera singer of fond memory. In charity they engaged her as their cook and housekeeper, relegating her to an equal share in their benevolent but gloomy religious routine. It was not until still many years later that the servant, Babette, was given the opportunity to reveal the culinary talents that had made her famous in Paris and, in so doing, she also reveals the true meaning of life, love, and the gift of self. Let us now see just how this mystery unfolds.

As the film opens, we are first struck by the image of the Jutland coast. Remote and desolate, yet magnificently unspoiled and intact, the setting embodies the *elemental*. Could there be a better environment for the emergence of the *essential?*

Next, we see a prayer group, whose members, we learn, are the disciples of a religious mentor long-since dead. This mentor, who had founded the sect, had been both feared and respected during his lifetime, but, with the passage of time the number of his disciples has diminished considerably.

The group is meeting for the purpose of "interpreting" the Word. They share a sober meal. In the kitchen, we see Babette preparing this frugal, insipid refection. Why? Because that is the full extent of what her employers have asked of her. Philippa and Martina, the daughters of the deceased master, lead the sect. They sing a hymn to God before the meal: "Never would you give a stone to your children who asked for bread" (Mt 7:9).

The atmosphere speaks volumes. We are confronted with a soulless, but undoubtedly sincere religious spirit, which is sterile and rigid. The Word, unsavored and unassimilated, is nonetheless "interpreted," but is this interpretation enough to nourish the *heart?* Their master is dead; so too, it appears, is their religion. The group reminds us of the "death of God" philosophy of the Existentialists and the death of God that occurs in the hearts of so many believers. Theirs is a "dead god," honored by a dead religion.

Everything is exterior, devoid of authenticity, mechanical, and robotic. Nevertheless, there is a presence *other* than that of the former master, whose portrait, still hanging on the wall, oversees their gatherings. That presence, Babette, could almost be called a Christ-figure. She is a "culinary genius," capable of nourishing these people with the finest foods, yet all that is asked of her, all that is expected of her, is to supplement their pious diet with dried bread. No, God does *not* give a stone to his children who ask for bread. But if the children ask for more, is God capable of satisfying their hunger—their spiritual hunger, their hunger for true Life, their hunger for God? The risk of inconveniencing God by asking for more is not taken. Babette remains marginalized by their ritual, the servant of their meager expectations!

One could argue that the *elemental* had not succeeded in revealing the *essential* to these good people! And yet, the seed is there, buried deep in the earth, waiting. The ambiance does seem to have an effect on the young lieutenant, whose superiors have sequestered him there against his will to give him time to reflect on the meaning of his life. Love for Martina opened his eyes to the *essential*, and he had "a mighty vision of a higher and purer life." This was equally true for the opera singer. Plunged into silence by the sound of crashing waves, he became depressed at the vanity of his fame. His hope was renewed upon hearing the voice of Philippa, which was to him the voice of a "diva." The *essential* surfaced for both men, but obstacles on the path to its attainment dissuaded them from pursuing it. How many people have abandoned the quest for the *essential* for fear its demands would be too great?

As for the sect, one gets the strong impression that their God is so transcendent as to forestall any immediate knowledge, relegating humankind to a distant dialogue. They know God to be Holy and Absolute, but to them God's ways are entirely inscrutable. As their hymn says, God is "beyond the mountains and the rivers." They devote themselves to disinterested, self-effacing adoration of this distant, yet imposing God. They believe that in Jesus this awesome God gave his life *for* us, but never consider God's desire to give his life *to* us! Immanence is unacknowledged; Emmanuel, *God-with-us*, is never experienced. Yet all is not hopeless, because in the person of Babette, the "stranger" has knocked at the door, seeking refuge in their *hearts* and offering to become their "servant." "If you will not permit me to be your servant, I will die," Babette had told the sisters. Hesitantly, they answered, "Stay with us." Entering, she dwelt with them.

Without wishing to force the analogy, I see in this initial abasement of Babette, in her willingness to assume the role of a servant, an echo of the Incarnation, the "first stage," as it were, of Christ's *kenosis:* ". . . he emptied himself, to assume the condition of a slave, and became as human beings are" (Ph 2:7). She spent fourteen years serving them, cloaked in the anonymity of a hidden and humble life. And yet, strangely enough, subtle changes took place in the lives of those who benefitted from Babette's services. The sisters were perplexed at discovering that their expenses had not increased since they hired Babette but, on the contrary, there was now money left over! Somewhat reminiscent of the jar of meal and the jug of oil used by the widow to provide for Elijah during the famine, their funds never diminished. Already, Babette's presence was enriching others, ever so discreetly.

The day of decision arrived along with ten thousand francs won in the lottery. Incomprehensibly, in place of the legitimate joy that this newly acquired wealth offered her, Babette chose to go to the depths of her joy by giving the best of herself for the joy of others. The hour of ultimate *kenosis* had arrived, a paschal *kenosis.* Clasping the crucifix that hung upon her breast, she asked the sisters' permission to prepare a "special meal" for the group. Reluctantly, the sisters accepted the offer, oblivious to what it would entail.

Preparations for Babette's feast get underway. No expense is too great; exotic food is imported. The culinary delights are of *another order.* The villagers watch from afar but everything is so far beyond their experience that they are not even capable of appreciating its true value. The members of the religious sect are both scandalized and fearful at the prospect of this so-called "French dinner." She has gone too far, they mutter; this is too much. It is blasphemous, diabolic! The "offer" is misunderstood, the "gift" scorned, the "feast" perceived as a risk. They close themselves to the mystery that is beyond them, making a pact among themselves to partake of the feast but not to enjoy it. They will act "as if they had no sense of taste." And, in fact, that is the case. The spiritual senses of their dormant *hearts* have atrophied through lack of stimulation. They are incapable of discerning the true nature of the reality confronting them. They do not know what God is offering them, and, what is worse, they do not want to know. Yet, once again, grace is stronger than death, and the gift offered is stronger than the refusal to receive it. They come to the feast, they consume fine foods and imbibe fine wine. Only one of them has "the sense" to marvel at the menu. Only one of the guests is astonished and ravished: the lieutenant of long ago, now a general, and returned for a final visit. I am reminded of the centurion of the gospel story, that stranger amid the crowd who alone had the necessary faith to recognize the true identity of Jesus.

In the course of the dinner, a subtle yet irresistible metamorphosis takes place: closed *hearts* open, hardened *hearts* soften, and sleeping *hearts* awaken. Grace does its work and the gift is now accepted with gratitude. Indeed, God has not given a stone to those who asked for bread; God gives God's self, without measure. "Everything is possible for God!" (Mk 10:27). By the time they leave the banquet, the congregation is of one heart and one soul; they form a circle around the well, singing and dancing their love. They have all drawn from the same wellspring, the source of living waters, and now their *hearts* overflow with joy! Their contact with the mercy of God, the abundance of God's grace, and the *real* in the spiritual life has really transformed them.

And what of Babette? She now reveals to the two sisters who she really is: the head "chef" at the renowned Café Anglais in Paris. She also admits to them that she has spent the entire ten thousand francs on the feast. Philippa and Martina are at once amazed and upset. "You should not have given all you own for us! Now, you will be poor the rest of your life." Babette tells them that artists are never poor when afforded the opportunity to give the very best of their art. No, those who give of their *being* are never impoverished by the gift, but, on the contrary, are enriched.

Babette is an icon of the person who has developed her innate "capacity" to the highest degree and who, having thus become the "great artist" God meant her to be, finds her joy in freely sharing the fruit of this plenitude. Is this not the journey we should all be on? We too, must develop our innate "capacity"—not for the culinary arts, the plastic arts, or any art of this kind, but for the "spiritual art." The noblest expression of this art form is not to create something but to *become* something, to *become* someone: the "saint" that God has meant us to *be* from all eternity.

Babette articulates the cry of the artist: "Throughout the world sounds one long cry from the heart of the artist: Give me the chance to do my very best!" In this I hear the cry of the monk: "Give me the chance to *become* my very best!" Monastic life provides the environment in which, by the grace of God, we can participate in the *feast* and enter into contact with the *other order*. This *other order* can bring about in us the metamorphosis from "image to likeness," empowering us to become fully who we are.

None of this is magic, if perhaps the film or my synopsis would create that impression. It is sanctity. Sanctity, although certainly "miraculous," does not emerge automatically, not even within an environment consecrated to that end. Like a stone immersed in water, we can be immersed in the world of grace while still remaining quite impervious to it. I am reminded of a diatribe of Charles Péguy in which, as one commentator stated, ". . . he demonstrates how one can create an impermeable envelope around oneself, which can successfully seal the soul against any penetration by grace."[2] It is a long excerpt but I think it is worth citing.[3]

He begins with a French pun which is lost in English, saying that all human beings are "weighable" but not necessarily "wet-able" (by which he means "penetrable"). He uses this pun

---

2. Pierre Miquel, *Lexique du Désert: Etude de Quelques Mots-Clés du Vocabulaire Monastique Grec Ancien*. Collection Spiritualité Orientale et Vie Monastique 44 (Bégrolles-en-Mauges [Maine-&-Loire]: Abbaye de Bellefontaine, 1986) 107.

3. It would be presumptuous of me to attempt an integral translation of Péguy's prose which is very intricate. I will intersperse paraphrase with literal translation.

to explain why grace sometimes appears to be lacking in effi-
cacy: ". . . winning victories in the soul of the greatest sinners,"
but often remaining inoperative ". . . in the most decent
people." How so? Because "decent people" or, rather, "those
who like to call themselves that," are clothed in the armor of
their virtue—thereby unwounded and morally intact.

> Their moral skin, constantly intact, becomes a leather hide
> and breastplate without defect. They do not present any
> opening that results from a frightful wound, an unforget-
> table distress, an invincible regret, an eternally unhealed
> scar, a mortal anxiety, or a secret bitterness . . . They do
> not present that opening to grace which is essentially what
> sin is. Because they are not wounded [by sin], they are not
> vulnerable either. Because they lack nothing, no one brings
> them anything. Because they lack nothing, no one brings
> them that which is everything. Even the charity of God
> does not bandage someone who has no wound . . . Some-
> one who has not fallen will never be picked up, and one
> who is not dirty will never be washed. "Decent people"
> don't get wet from grace.[4]

Continuing in this vein, he compares morality to a sort of
resin that coats the skin of the supposedly just people, rendering them impermeable to grace. Grace can transform the greatest criminals and the most miserable sinners, first and foremost
because it can penetrate them; it can get under their skin. It can
get inside and work its wonders. Not so with the "decent" folk
who cannot absorb any "moisture" (i.e., grace) through their
impenetrable moral epidermis.

> That is why nothing is so contrary to what we name reli-
> gion as what we name morality. And nothing is so asinine
> . . . as to put the two together. One can almost say that, on
> the contrary, all that is taken by grace is taken away from
> morality. And that all that is won over by the name of
> morality, all that is coated with the name of morality, is by
> that very fact . . . impenetrable to grace.[5]

4. Quote cited in Miquel 107–108.
5. Miquel, 108.

If one subscribes to his interpretation, one would rightly assert that what is lacking in religion is certainly not "grace"; on the contrary, "Wisdom has set her table" and all are invited to share it. In order to transform us, however, grace needs an opening. This opening is to be found in our indigence rather than in our "moral feats." God awaits us in the "faille"—the weak point, the fragility, "the fault"—of our *being*, and will inundate us with grace—gratuitously. Eventually, Babette's feast brought those who feasted down into this "fault," into this zone of vulnerability where one can be penetrated by the mercy of God.

I readily admit the possibility that my words, as necessary as they may have been in this context, have succeeded only in obscuring the impact of the drama unfurled before us. By the very atmosphere that permeates its every aspect—an atmosphere that is elemental in beauty and potential as well as in the bleakness of its mien—the story speaks more eloquently than words can utter. The religious sect merges with the bleakness; Babette, however, redeems its barrenness with a *being* capable of responding to an unarticulated yet pervasive anticipation. Her *being* remains hidden for a long time before the opportunity comes to manifest itself through its effects. Yet, even then, Babette herself abides in obscurity. A transformation takes place around her, but she remains out of the limelight. She empties herself and sacrifices herself to give life and joy to others. She is like the *hollow* whence *new life* surges and grace flows freely, penetrating open *hearts:* a perfect icon of what the monk is called to *be!*

8

SOULSCAPE

As is no doubt evident by now, my approach to delving into the mystery of *spiritual being* differs from the methodology of a doctrinal treatise. The latter approach could surely be taken, and fruitfully so, for there is a wealth of theological and spiritual doctrine that would provide a more objective basis for this subject; but I have chosen to explore my theme from a more subjective vantage point, using symbols, images, literature, and even cinematography as channels of intuition. This "methodology," which may appear to be somewhat unorthodox, is characteristic of my own spiritual journey and has served me well over the years. My concern here is to focus on the unique person who is involved in the journey toward *spiritual being*. To attain the goal it is essential that each individual discover *his/her* path within *the* path, *his/her* journey within *the* journey. I call this "finding one's soulscape" amidst the horizons of a more objective spiritual landscape.

Our objective landscape would be the Cistercian vocation, with its distinctive lifestyle and patrimony. We are immersed in this landscape as unique persons. While the characteristic features of the objective landscape do not vary all that much, the individual living within it should have a unique identity, a proper "face." Ours is not a faceless journey on which the individual must meld into a Cistercian mold that fabricates a monastic *persona* instead of a monastic person. Our vocation is at once common and personal. I call the personal face of this journey-within-a-journey, this unique journey within a common journey, the *soulscape.*

Each of us is unique. Individual histories vary considerably. God instructs us in our lives by means of the mysterious synergy of grace and our free response to it. All of these factors converge, influencing the dynamics at work within our particular monastic journey. Consequently, an interior vision of a highly personal tenor should quite naturally emerge along the way. Such a vision provides a schema by which one can articulate the goal of the journey and discern the most appropriate means of arriving at it.

Following this line of thought, it could be said that Christianity is itself a vision—a life-vision—and that our Cistercian charism is a vision within that larger vision. As monks, we need to explore the length, the breadth, the depths, and the heights of both visions, yet from the perspective of our own personal charism within them. And is it not true that the "life of faith" basically amounts to the conscious nurturing of an existential, grounded, personal vision of a body of revealed truths? We could spend a lifetime assimilating and understanding the implications and nuances inherent in such a vision. In so doing, we would be appropriating it and incarnating it in our own unique fashion.

The emergent personal or interior vision harmonizes and clarifies what could otherwise become an overwhelming plethora of spiritual data which could so overload us that we could wade through but only insufficiently absorb it. Initially, the more objective faith-vision, whether that of the Church or that of the monastic tradition, may seem a jumble of disparate dogmas and doctrines. Yet, little by little, by journeying within this landscape, we make it our own, and a more subjective synthesis coalesces. As we walk in the light that begins to shine on our path, as we deepen our attention and refine our receptivity, as we struggle to incarnate the truth known at a given moment, as we open wide our *heart* to the vastness of the horizon unfolding before us, this vision can become a consuming fire and a constraining desire! This inner vision inspires and energizes us, giving ultimate meaning to our life and itself becoming a source of fuller life.

Rest assured that I am not advocating eccentricity or originality—one's spiritual vision should be firmly rooted in one's doctrinal and spiritual tradition. Yet if an individual's journey is to bear fruit within this more objective context, means must be found and taken for making it his/her own. This is a matter not of contorting or distorting the objective realities, but rather of appropriating them. Our soulscape should be intimately linked to the Cistercian landscape, thus giving it a soul. An affinity exists between the soulscape and the landscape, this secret connection is undoubtedly present in seminal form at the outset of a monastic vocation but it requires cultivation throughout a lifetime. The soulscape is the secret connection between the depth of the person and the depth of the milieu.

A soulscape is born within the actual context of the journey. It is neither invented nor artificially manufactured; it is an interior echo of the journey that vivifies, unifies, and clarifies it. Once it sounds, this interior echo must be listened to and tended, so that we can formulate our own articulation of the Word and make the journey our own. At this point there is ample possibility for freedom and spontaneity. The soulscape of the journey reveals a more personal and intimate topography.

We must respect and nurture our traditional Cistercian lifestyle and patrimony, and we must safeguard our Cistercian landscape to ensure its integrity. At the same time, however, we must allow the unique person within each of us to emerge and within this landscape to become an equally integral part of the Cistercian reality. All this is merely a manner of transposing the principle of inculturation to a more personal dimension. In both scenarios, lifestyle becomes identity through this mysterious union of landscape and soulscape, which, far from attenuating the Cistercian experience, enhances and intensifies it.

To return to the image of sculpting that was mentioned earlier: it has been said that the artist who does not make his or her own tools, does not make his or her own sculpture. The soulscape is our personal tool for penetrating ever more deeply the spiritual realities that constitute the substance of our monastic life. This precious tool enables us to keep on journeying, inspired by the ardent hope that "in another few days," *being* will break through!

Looking at these matters from a practical point of view, one might well ask how to go about appropriating or personalizing the more objective aspects of the journey to *spiritual being*. My response would be: by having recourse to one's own inner capacities and attractions, by being open and attentive to the delicate vibrations of the *heart*, and by refining one's receptivity to the messages transmitted by the spiritual "antennas"—all of which can be vehicles of grace, attuning us to the subtle solicitations of *being* that are present on our path. Of course, the sensitivity particular to each person differs. I have spoken of the images and symbols that are the marrow of my journey-within-a-journey. Yet this is just one modality, one soulscape; I take this approach because it is the one with which I am most familiar. Nonetheless, I would imagine that there are as many "variations on the theme" as there are individuals committed to a journey.

Allow me to expand briefly on some of the particularities (if not peculiarities!) of my own soulscape, peppered as it is with a variety of symbols and images. It may provide you with a clue for deciphering what must at times seem enigmatic.

In the spiritual realm which is enmeshed in mystery, it is often difficult, if not impossible, to grasp or communicate certain realities on a purely rational level. Take, for example, the account of Amadeus' transformation in *Missa sine Nomine*. Insight into the subtle, intangible nature of his spiritual metamorphosis was provided by the equally subtle use of the music of Mozart as a symbol of this mysterious interior process. Images and symbols can play a very important role. Appearing almost spontaneously at certain moments, they are often instrumental in shaping the evolution of a journey. They help one grasp more firmly what has been discovered or experienced, and they project light onto the road that lies ahead. This approach is in harmony with monastic spirituality for, as one author describes it:

> The language of monastic theology is quite distinctive. There is a conscious attempt to limit theological utterance to image and symbol out of respect for the mystery of God, for the limits that God's ineffability naturally creates.[1]

1. Aidan Nichols, *The Shape of Catholic Theology* (Collegeville, MN: The Liturgical Press, 1991) 289.

It is, nonetheless, a fact that images and symbols cannot always do justice to the reality signified, especially within the spiritual world. I mentioned that prayer, depth, *spiritual being*, and transformation are mysteries to be contemplated, and that is precisely what we have been doing: employing symbols and images of the most varied sort (sculpture, music, censers, potatoes—cooked and raw—stones, seashells, and *haute cuisine*) to help us sound their depths. And yet, because of the very nature of the realities being considered, the limitations of symbols as symbols are acutely felt. Symbols, even the most sublime, fall short of grasping and adequately transmitting the very mystery intuited and suggested by them. As beautiful as the symbol or image may be, the reality far surpasses it. Forewarned of these limitations, something which is capable of putting us, however remotely, in contact with such elusive realities is nevertheless a graced experience.

Despite these inescapable limitations, symbols and images can sometimes transport us to unsuspected depths. Just how or why is difficult to know. Perhaps it is because they themselves issue from a depth within the person and so can lead to even further depths. Perhaps it is because there is a vast interior space within the human person where the reality signified by the symbol or image can reverberate: this space is what we have been calling the deep *heart*. The *heart* harbors unfathomed spiritual depths of infinite resonance. I would go so far as to say, with the French Dominican theologian, Fr. Régamey, that our deepest truth, our truest self, is not to be found in the intellect, the passions, or the will, but rather in the *heart*, which is the most intimate region of our *being*, deeper than our ideas, sentiments, and willful deliberations. It is here that we discover the most fundamental dynamism of our nature: we are made for God and the *élan*, the impulse, toward God inscribed in our *heart* constitutes the very essence of our *being*.[2]

Another way of referring to this profound interior reservoir of spiritual life would be to borrow Saint Augustine's concept

---

2. R. Régamey, *Portrait Spirituel du Chrétien* (Paris: Éditions du Cerf, 1963) 50–51.

of *memoria*. The *memoria*, one of the faculties of the soul in his anthropology, contains the imprint of the presence of God. In exploring the influence of Saint Augustine on William of Saint Thierry, David Bell wrote:

> *Memoria*, as Père Javelet has it, is "an existential *rapport* of the soul with God." It is not simply a mental function directed towards the past, but the latent presence of God in the soul, and (what comes to the same thing) the latent participation of the soul in God. Memory provides man with a certain innate knowledge of God which remains to be actualized, to be made explicit, as Cayré puts it, and it acts as a force driving him on towards its realization.[3]

Any and all means that will help us tap into and actualize the latent content of this inner world of the deep *heart*, or *memoria*, are of inestimable value on our journey toward *spiritual being*, for, as we said, consciousness and *being* are intimately connected. Even though the parallel is not exact, I am reminded of the importance accorded to the concept of the "collective unconscious" by Carl Gustav Jung. Jung believed that one of the reasons the modern age is so singularly bereft of spirit is that we no longer live a symbolic life. With this I emphatically agree. Symbols and images serve to awaken the *heart*, causing it to vibrate and resonate, thereby signaling to all who have ears to hear, the presence of unsuspected or neglected spiritual spheres inherent in human nature. In this way, depths are disclosed, spiritual consciousness grows, and *spiritual being* blossoms.

---

3. David N. Bell, *Image and Likeness: The Augustinian Spirituality of William of Saint Thierry*. Cistercian Studies Series 78 (Kalamazoo, MI: Cistercian Publications, 1984) 26. In this passage, Bell quotes Robert Javelet, *Image et Ressemblance au XIIe Siècle: de Saint Anselme à Alain de Lille*. 2 vols. (Paris: Letouzey et Ané, 1967) 1:60 and Fulbert Cayré, *La Contemplation Augustinienne: Principes de Spiritualité et de Théologie*, rev. ed. (Bruges: Desclée de Brouwer, 1954) 181.

CONCLUSION

We have arrived at the end of this retreat but not at the end of the journey. The journey of the monk is a never-ending quest for God. And, as I said at the outset, we are not just *on* a journey: we ourselves *are* the journey. This is essentially an interior journey, a quest that leads into the depths of the *heart*. As monks, we are well aware that it is not necessary to travel far and wide on our search for God. What is necessary is to *return to* the heart, to sink down into our inner depths. I recall the poignant story of a musk deer who expended all his time and energy seeking the traces of the essential everywhere except where it was—in his own heart. Listen carefully to the tale:

> One day many years ago, the musk deer of the mountains sniffed a breath of musked perfume. He leaped from jungle to jungle in pursuit of the musk. The poor animal no longer ate, or drank, or slept. He didn't know where the scent of the musk came from, but he was impelled to pursue it through ravines, forests and hills. Finally, starving, harassed, exhausted and wandering about at random, he slipped from the top of a rock and fell mortally wounded.
>
> The musk deer's last act before he died was to take pity on himself and lick his breast. And his musk pouch, torn when he fell on the rock, poured out its perfume. He gasped and tried to breathe in the perfume, but it was too late. Beloved son, don't seek the perfume of God outside yourself, and perish in the jungle of life. Search your soul and look within. He will be there.[1]

1. Henri Caffarel, *Being Present to God: Letters on Prayer,* translated by Angeline Bouchard (New York: Society of St. Paul, 1983) 166.

The beginning of the final stanza of T. S. Eliot's "Little Gidding" comes immediately to mind:

> We shall not cease from exploration
> And the end of all exploring
> Will be to arrive where we started
> And know the place for the first time.[2]

After all our explorations during this retreat, you may well be thinking: "What a strange Cistercian! She did not refer to a single Cistercian Father or Mother, or to the Rule of Saint Benedict!" Or, worse yet, perhaps you are even thinking: "What a strange Christian! She hardly touched on Scripture! She makes reference to all sorts of other things—and an odd array of things at that!"

I would hope that, nonetheless, you would now have a somewhat sympathetic understanding of my manner of approaching these topics. I did not come to you armed with scholarly discourses on Cistercian spirituality, the Rule, or theological issues. I have offered nought but my "widow's mite"; it may not be much, but it is all I have!

My soulscape began taking shape when a "sense" awakened in me, setting me on a quest to find the source of a "presence." Somewhat akin to the musk deer seduced by a perfumed scent, I was attentive and responsive to everything along the way that stimulated and refined this "sense." The patristic and Cistercian doctrine of the human person as "image and likeness of God" helped to clarify my initial intuition, and the doctrine of the *"heart"* oriented my search toward the interior spaces. The Incarnation spoke to me of divinization. The mystery drew me then and continues to draw me now. It is everywhere—in the liturgy, the Word of God, monastic values, monastic vows, Rule, and spirituality; but its presence is also manifest in people, literature, art, sculpture, music, film, nature, matter, science—everywhere—and it calls to me. A vision has evolved as the

---

2. T. S. Eliot, *Four Quartets* (New York: Harcourt, Brace and Company, 1943) 39.

horizon has become ever more vast: soulscape is immersed in landscape seeking the frontiers of *another order!*

The table has been set. The "banquet" has been served. Unfortunately it is not "*à la* Babette"—I have never been much of a cook, let alone a culinary artist! I thank you for affording me the chance to "give my very best" and to "sound the depths of my joy" in the sharing of these thoughts with you.

INDEX

CISTERCIAN PUBLICATIONS

Cistercian Publications publishes books in four series—Cistercian Fathers, Cistercian Studies, Cistercian Liturgy, and Monastic Wisdom—and in the following areas:

MONASTIC TEXTS IN ENGLISH TRANSLATION

• Sermons and treatises by twelfth & thirteenth-century cistercian spiritual writers
• Classic texts from the monastic wisdom of both the eastern and western Churches

MONASTIC LIFE, HISTORY, SPIRITUALITY, ARCHITECTURE, AND LITURGY

• For those with a personal interest in contemplative prayer and monastic lifestyle
• For students exploring monastic tradition
• For scholars specializing in aspects of monastic history, art, liturgy, or theology

• Reflections by contemporary monks and nuns
• Specialized studies by scholars
• Overviews of patristic & medieval doctrine
• Cistercian music and retreat addresses on CD and audio-cassette
• Video / DVD visits to contemporary abbeys

Editorial Offices & Customer Service

• Cistercian Publications: Editorial Offices
WMU Station, 1903 West Michigan Avenue
Kalamazoo, Michigan 49008-5415   USA

Telephone   269 387 8920
Fax   269 387 8390
e-mail   cistpub@wmich.edu

• Cistercian Publications: Customer Service
Liturgical Press
Saint John's Abbey
Collegeville, MN 56321-7500

Telephone   800 436 8431
Fax   320 363 3299
e-mail   sales@litpress.org

Canada

• Bayard-Novalis
49 Front Street East, Second Floor
Toronto, Ontario M5E 1B3   CANADA

Telephone   800 387 7164
Fax   416 363 9409

UK and Europe

• The Columba Press
55A Spruce Avenue
Stillorgan Industrial Park
Blackrock, Co. Dublin   Ireland

Telephone   353 1 2942556
Fax   353 1 2942564
e-mail   info@columba.ie

Website

• www.cistercianpublications.org

To explore the range of titles in our series of texts and studies in the monastic tradition, please request our free complete catalogue from customer service or visit our website.